SHREWD FOOD

Elizabeth Carty was born in Ireland but has spent most of her adult life abroad. She has had a lifelong interest in food, owing her initial palate development to her mother, whom she describes as a fine cook with a modest repertoire. Later, during her time living in London, Cyprus and Dubai, she was introduced to a wide array of cuisine styles, which influence her cooking today.

She returned to Ireland with her son in 2000. A recent divorcee, she had to adjust to life on significantly reduced means. She worked by day and studied at night, qualifying as an accountant in 2006. Her love of cooking and entertaining, and her knowledge of doing so on a tight budget, led her to found the Shrewd Food website, with her son, in 2009. It has generated a huge response from enthusiastic foodies both in Ireland and abroad.

Shrewd Food is her first book.

SHREWD FOOD

A New Way of Shopping, Cooking and Eating

Elizabeth Carty

HACHETTE
BOOKS
IRELAND

First published in 2010 by Hachette Books Ireland
A division of Hachette UK Ltd.

1

A CIP catalogue record for this title is available from the British Library.

ISBN 978 1 444 70495 2

Inside design by Sin É Design
Printed and bound in Great Britain by CPI Mackays, Chatham ME5 8TD

Hachette Books Ireland policy is to use papers that are natural, renewable
and recyclable products and made from wood grown in sustainable forests.
The logging and manufacturing processes are expected to conform to the
environmental regulations of the country of origin.

Hachette Books Ireland
8 Castlecourt Centre
Castleknock
Dublin 15, Ireland
A division of Hachette UK Ltd
338 Euston Road
London NW1 3BH

www.hachette.ie

CONTENTS

To Mother, whose cooking gave me an early-life introduction to excellent, home-cooked food, who taught me how to shop shrewdly, and whose 'can-do' approach to life has always inspired me.

INTRODUCTION

I am a third generation 'shrewdie'. My grandmother was a shrewdie. While her circumstances were comfortable – they had a shop in Dublin and a farm in the country – from what I know of her, she was a prudent and careful housewife. My mother, one of the most generous people I've known, was also a shrewdie. To use one of her own phrases, she could live on 'the clippings of tin'. Nothing was ever wasted in our house. I learned the shrewd lesson very early on in life. When I say I come from a long line of shrewdies, my pedigree is impeccable.

I lived for several years abroad, mainly in London, Cyprus and Dubai. I have had a lifelong passion for good food and it has always featured significantly on my travels. Wherever I went I sought out good places to eat. I met people from all over the world, particularly in London and Dubai, both melting pots of different nationalities, and food was always a shared interest. Everywhere I went I cooked and swapped recipes and food ideas with friends and acquaintances.

When I returned to Ireland in 2000 I was facing a lot of change. I was recently divorced, with a young child and an ex-husband with financial problems. If ever I needed my shrewd living skills, this was the time. I bought a big freezer and budgeted very seriously. I took maximum advantage of special offers. When food was reduced, I bought in bulk. I put fresh food in the freezer and stored the rest. I remember getting to the checkout of my local supermarket, with six half-price rib roasts, then spending about an hour trying to fit the booty in the freezer!

The combination of careful budgeting and creative cooking meant that we lived comfortably and we always ate well. Over the years of travel and shared interest in food, I have learned that food does not have to be expensive to be good. Cheap and simple ingredients can often provide the basis for a wealth of delicious and nutritious dishes, and special offers can cover the rest.

When the recession came along, a lot of people found that they could no longer afford to pick things off the supermarket shelf without a glance at the price. As a consequence, special offers became an important part of the shopping trip for many. I started the shrewdfood.ie website to share my experience with others, and it is out of this that the book has grown.

You can make maximum use of the recipes by using the book alongside the website www.shrewdfood.ie, which is regularly updated with information on special offers and taste testing/value assessments across the supermarket chains and brands. A significant number of supermarket special offers are repeated frequently and the majority of the recipes in this book are based on those offers.

But budgeting aside, I think that it's hugely important to enjoy cooking. We have to eat and most of us will spend a fair amount of time in the preparation of food, so it is worth putting a little effort into it and enjoying the journey. I get bored with cooking the same dishes all the time and I like to try new recipes when time permits. There are recipes in this book from all over the world and I've had fun discovering them – I hope you will enjoy that discovery too.

Notes on recipes

Variations: *Where appropriate, recipes offer leaner, child-friendly and gluten-free options, abbreviated at the end of recipes as follows:*

Leaner: L

Child-friendly: C-F

Gluten-free: G-F

Stock: *Homemade stock is almost always better than any you can buy, and if time permits I would recommend making your own – see stock recipes on pages 228 and 229. Where a recipe calls for strong stock I would boil a stock down to reduce it by half. Where a recipe states extra strong stock I would reduce the liquid by two-thirds. I am happy to use stock cubes or store-bought stock for everyday cooking and I would reduce the quantity of water to stock as appropriate. We did a taste testing of stock cubes for the Shrewd Food website and the results are available on www.shrewdfood.ie in the section titled 'The Panel'.*

Servings: *Unless otherwise stated, recipes serve four.*

SHREWD
BUYING

've been a shrewd shopper all my life. I've always been of the opinion that one can eat very well very cheaply and that, with a little thought and planning, one can save a lot of money on food. I love shopping and anything saved on food can be spent elsewhere – or even saved! So listed below are some tips and ideas that will help optimise those weekly bargains and make the most of each shopping trip.

Buying food that's in season (and locally produced where possible) makes sense for many reasons. Seasonal food is usually great value, the produce is at its best, and buying local generally means that the food is fresher. It also means less 'food miles', which contributes to a greener earth. See page 9 for a seasonal chart of commonly eaten fruit and vegetables.

SHREWD SHOPPING TIPS

* **PLAN YOUR MENU AND YOUR SHOPPING LIST**
Find out what the special offers are before you plan. You can get these from junk mail that arrives in your letterbox, from newspaper advertisements or from supermarket websites. The shrewdfood.ie website updates its listings of specials in each supermarket every week and provides recipes for some of the specials. If you have a choice of supermarket, decide which has the best offers and save on motor fuel or transport. Without planning, special offers can actually increase the shopping bill – how easy it is to be tempted by low prices to buy things that we don't need, and which often end up in the bin because they go bad before we get to cook them.

*   **STICK TO THE LIST**

You get to the shop and you see something reduced for clearance – unless you are sure you can fit it into the menu plan, or freeze it (labels usually have a blue logo that indicates an item can be frozen and all fresh meat and vegetables can be frozen – see section below on freezing), don't buy it, no matter how cheap it is. It's not cheap if you are buying it to bin it. And this leads on the next point . . .

*   **FREEZE**

If you have a freezer, and have space in it, bulk buy a really good offer and freeze it. Do check that it can be frozen (see Shrewd Freezer section for guidelines) and for how long, and make sure that you will be able to eat them all before the freezer sell-by date. Consider also buying extra, cooking it and freezing the cooked dish. This not only saves you money. On a day when you don't feel like cooking or haven't got the time, it is great to be able to defrost and heat up something from the freezer.

*   **SNACK BEFORE YOU SHOP**

To avoid temptation, it's not a good idea to go shopping when hungry. Hunger makes everything look delicious, which leads to a tendency to overbuy. Shopping when you are hungry can also make you tired and irritable, therefore less capable of making rational decisions. So if you are hungry, have something to eat. Even a piece of fruit on the hoof will take the edge off your hunger and give you the energy boost you need to make the best shopping choices.

*   **BE CRITICAL OF OFFERS**

Not all specials are good value. Very expensive items, even with a discount, can still be very expensive and outside your budget.

*   **SHOP EARLY**

If possible, shop early. Many shops put out a quota of specials per day and these often sell out quickly. Some specials are on a 'while stocks last' basis and once all the stocks have sold the offer is off, so it's best to buy when the offer is first published.

* **ASK AND THOU SHALT RECEIVE**

Not all special offers are prominently displayed in the shop. The item on sale may be what's called a 'loss leader', which means the shop is taking a loss on that item in order draw people to that particular supermarket and stimulate other profitable sales. So if you can't find the offer, ask a shop assistant where it is. I know one of the major supermarkets that frequently has meat offers but only makes them available at the meat counter: they do not appear on the shelves at all.

* **BUY VALUE PRODUCTS**

Value products are usually less expensive than popular brands. They are often of very good quality and can, on occasion, be better than well-known popular brands. Check out The Panel section on the www.shrewdfood.ie website for reviews of many everyday value products.

* **LOOK AT THE SMALL PRINT**

Not all special offers are available in all the branches of a particular store, so look at the small print. If you have a choice of branch, pick the biggest as this will be most likely to have all the offers.

* **WATCH THE PACKING**

Look out for packages that are different sizes and weights from what you normally buy. I often see special offers that are in larger or smaller packs than usual, but when I calculate the unit or base cost per kilo, I find that they are just as expensive, or even more so, than the everyday price. It's a good idea to have a small calculator with you when you shop – I have one that's the size of a credit card and I find it very useful.

* **WATCH THE QUALITY**

Sometimes food is sold off cheaply because it is beginning to go bad – by the time you have discarded any bad items, the price might not be any better than the normal one.

* **COMPARE LIKE WITH LIKE**

Look out for goods in different stages of preparation. Unprepared foods might look very cheap – e.g. peas in the pod, meat on the bone or whole fish – but when you have shelled the peas, boned the meat and taken the head, fins and tail off the fish, how does the price compare with items in a similar state of preparation for cooking?

*   **IS THREE FOR THE PRICE OF TWO BETTER THAN ONE?**
Do you really need three tubs of fresh cream or twenty kilograms of potatoes? Might they go bad before you get to use them up?

*   **BUY FRESH PRODUCE SUCH AS TOMATOES, POTATOES, SALAD ETC., ONLY WHEN YOU NEED THEM**
– they taste much better fresh and there is less likelihood of waste.

*   **WATCH THE SELL-BY DATE**
Pick items that have the longest sell-by date. These are often at the back of the shelf or on the highest or lowest shelves. The food will be fresher and will last longer, reducing the likelihood of waste due to spoilage.

In summary I would say that, when dealing with supermarkets, my general rule of thumb would be *caveat emptor* – let the buyer beware. Supermarkets have a host of professional marketing people at their disposal, who understand the psychology of selling and of the shopper, and their aim is to sell, sell, sell and understandably so – they are in business to make money. Being aware of this is the first step on the road to better buying. To borrow from and rephrase Thomas Jefferson – the price of good shopping is constant vigilance.

SHREWD SEASONS

Fruits in Season

Apples	September to January
Blackberries	July to October
Blueberries	June to September
Cherries	May to July
Cranberries	November to December
Gooseberries	June to July
Peaches	July to September
Pears	September to January
Plums	August to October
Raspberries	June to September
Strawberries	May to July
Tomatoes	June to October

Vegetables in Season

Asparagus	April to June
Aubergine	May to October
Broccoli	July to October
Brussels sprouts	October to February
Cabbage	All the year round
Carrot	May to October
Celery – white – green	 August to February All year round

Vegetables in Season cont.

Chives	All the year round
Courgette	June to October
French Bean	July to September
Leeks	September to April
Lettuce	April to October
Mangetout	June to September
Marrow	July to November
Mushroom – field	 July to September
Onion	Most of the year
Parsnip	October to April
Peas	June to September
Potato	Main crop July to February but new potatoes come in around May
Pumpkin	August to December
Scallions	April to September
Spinach	April to September
Swede	September to March

THE SHREWD STORE CUPBOARD

We live in very busy times and I find it useful to keep a basic stock of food items that are regularly used, replacing items just before they run out. Each recipe in the book has a shopping list at the end, however I have assumed that the items in the store cupboard below are in stock and have not included them.

Shrewd staples

baking powder

basil, dried

bay leaves, dried

bicarbonate of soda (bread soda)

butter

cayenne powder

chilli powder

chillis, fresh – I buy these in an Asian shop, where they are very cheap, wash and dry them and put them in a plastic bag in a Tupperware container in the freezer. When I need a chilli, I remove one and run it under the cold tap for a minute to defrost it. Note: Plastic containers become very brittle when frozen and can break easily. To prevent the lid breaking on opening, run it under the hot tap for half a minute to defrost it before opening

cinnamon powder

cocktail sticks

coriander, ground

cornflour

cumin, ground

curry powder

eggs

flour, plain and self-raising

garlic, fresh

herbs, dried mixed

lemon, fresh

mayonnaise – for everyday use, I find it saves time to have a jar of good quality, store-bought mayonnaise in the fridge

milk

mint, dried

mustard powder

nutmeg, grated or whole

oil, corn, olive, peanut, sunflower

onions

oregano, dried

Oxo beef stock cubes

paprika

Parmesan cheese – can be grated and frozen in small quantities. However it is advisable not to keep it for too long in the freezer as it loses flavour quickly

pasta, large packet of dried

pepper, black peppercorns

pepper, white

potatoes

rice, **arborio** – for risotto

rice, **basmati** and/or ordinary long grain

rice, pudding

rosemary, dried

salt, table, cooking and rock or sea salt

soy sauce, light

spice, dried mixed

stock, beef, chicken, fish, vegetable

sugar, white, brown, caster and icing

Szechuan pepper

Tabasco sauce – great for a multitude of recipes that need heat, and essential in a Bloody Mary

thyme, dried

tin foil

tomato ketchup

tomato purée, tinned or in a tube

tomatoes, fresh – can be used in so many ways

turmeric powder

vanilla essence or extract

vinegar or cider vinegar and a good red wine vinegar

wine, white and red – suitable for cooking (you know what they say – if you can't drink it, don't cook with it)

Worcestershire sauce

SHREWD
SOUPS, STARTERS & HORS D'OEUVRES

Astarter is perfect as a light meal, but in these busy times few of us would make a starter on a daily basis. However, the starter is possibly the most important dish you will serve at a dinner party. To your guests it's an indication of many things – your culinary skills, the effort you have made on their behalf and what sort of standard they might expect for the rest of the meal. I tend to put my best foot forward for the starter, and when that's good, I find that everybody, guests and hosts alike, relaxes.

I'm a lover of soups, especially vegetable soups. They're healthy, easy to prepare, great value and a good way to add to our 'five a day'. Then there is the added benefit that if I have soup, I'm less likely to have a dessert!

Most soups can be prepared one or two days beforehand, which takes some of the pressure off on the day.

CAULIFLOWER SOUP

This delicious soup makes a hearty starter. To make ahead, prepare to the stage where the soup is liquidised. Just before serving, reheat gently to a simmer and stir in the cheese etc.

INGREDIENTS

50g butter

1 medium onion, chopped

2 stalks of celery, chopped

1 medium carrot, chopped

1 medium cauliflower, roughly chopped into bite-size pieces

1 tbsp freshly chopped parsley

700ml (3½ cups) vegetable or chicken stock or a mixture of both

1 tbsp cornflour, dissolved in 50ml (¼ cup) of milk

a few chopped chives or scallions to serve (optional)

1 tbsp grated mature Cheddar or any similar strong cheese (optional)

METHOD

1 Heat the butter in a saucepan, over a medium heat, until it begins to foam. Add the onion, celery and carrot and cook for a few minutes. Add the cauliflower and parsley, and increase the heat until the vegetables heat up, stirring to ensure they don't brown. Reduce the heat, cover with a lid and simmer very gently for 15 minutes, stirring occasionally.

2 Add the stock and bring to the boil. Reduce the heat, cover and simmer gently until the vegetables are cooked – about 10 minutes.

3 Add the milk and the cornflour mixture and simmer gently for about 5 minutes.

4 Remove from the heat and liquidise half the mixture. Return to the pot and mix with the un-liquidised soup. Reheat without boiling.

5 Sprinkle a few chopped chives or scallions on top and serve immediately.

Note: If serving as a main course, add the cheese just before serving and stir until it partially melts into the soup.

OPTIONS

Serve with crusty bread and butter.

L: Use 1 tbsp sunflower or corn oil instead of butter, use low-fat milk and don't add any cheese at the end. You could also leave out the cornflour and the milk altogether and have a lighter soup — either way, it's good!

C-F: Use medium instead of mature Cheddar.

G-F: Use gluten-free stock and check that the cheese used is gluten-free.

SHOPPING LIST

celery
carrots
cauliflower
parsley
fresh scallions or chives (to serve)
mature cheddar or similar strong cheese (to serve)

RED KIDNEY BEAN SOUP

Kidney beans, in common with most beans, are excellent value as well as being a good source of cholesterol-lowering fibre and, when combined with whole grains such as rice, provide a good source of protein that is also virtually fat free.

INGREDIENTS

30g butter

1 medium onion, chopped

2 medium carrots, chopped

1 clove of garlic, chopped

1 400ml tin of kidney beans, drained and rinsed

700ml (3½ cups) vegetable or chicken stock

a couple of sprigs of fresh thyme or ½ tsp dried thyme

¼-1 tsp chilli powder or cayenne pepper, according to taste

a few chopped chives or scallions, to serve

salt

SHOPPING LIST

carrots
tinned kidney beans
fresh thyme (optional – dried is fine)
chives or scallions (to serve)

METHOD

1 Heat the butter in a saucepan over a medium heat and sauté the onions, carrots and garlic for about 5 minutes until they are slightly golden.

2 Add the kidney beans, thyme, stock and cayenne. Bring to the boil and reduce the heat. Cover and simmer for about 45 minutes.

3 If it's your preference, liquidise and return to the pot. Reheat gently and serve with some chopped chives or scallions.

OPTIONS

A little boiled brown or white rice can be added to serve.

L: Use 2 tbsp oil instead of butter.

C-F: Make without chilli powder or cayenne.

G-F: Ensure stock, spices and vinegar are gluten-free.

CHINESE CHICKEN & SWEETCORN SOUP

Mmmm! This has long been a favourite of mine. It's gutsy enough to be a main course by increasing the amount of chicken, or you can leave the chicken out altogether for a lighter soup.

INGREDIENTS

1 chicken breast, chopped into fine strips, approx. 1cm

1 125g tin of sweetcorn, drained

500ml (2½ cups) chicken stock (Chinese use extra strong stock so if your stock is fresh, boil it down to reduce by about a half. If using stock cubes, adjust the amount of cubes to water, to taste)

3 heaped tsp cornflour, mixed with a little water

1 egg white, beaten

1 scallion, trimmed and chopped diagonally, for garnish (optional)

SHOPPING LIST

chicken breast fillet

tinned sweetcorn

METHOD

1 Put the drained sweetcorn and stock into a pot and bring to the boil.

2 Add the cornflour and stir until it thickens.

3 Add the chopped chicken strips, stir, and cook for a few minutes until it's cooked through.

4 Just before serving add the beaten egg white to the hot soup, whisking briskly with a fork, so that it cooks in white strands. Remove from the heat.

5 Put the soup into bowls and serve with a sprinkling of the chopped scallion.

OPTIONS

Serve with soy sauce on the side. A little boiled rice can be added for body.

C-F: For children who dislike the texture of sweetcorn, liquidise the soup.

G-F: Ensure stock is gluten-free.

BUTTERNUT SQUASH SOUP

When the orange, bell-shaped squashes arrive in the shops, I feel harvest has come and it's time to start stocking up for the winter. Butternut squash offers good value in autumn, and this lovely warming soup has a distinctively sweet, nutty taste. The squash can be roasted before making the soup, but I have given a simpler version here.

INGREDIENTS

45g butter

1 butternut squash, peeled, deseeded and cut into 1½cm cubes

1 carrot, scraped and chopped

2 small celery sticks, washed and cut into 1cm slices

1 large onion, chopped

1 litre (5 cups) chicken stock

a little grating of fresh nutmeg (just a pinch) or ¼ tsp cinnamon powder

100ml (½ cup) of cream or buttermilk to serve

salt and freshly ground black pepper

METHOD

1 Heat the butter in a saucepan over a medium heat. Add a little salt and sauté the onions, carrot and celery gently, until soft – approx. 7 minutes. Add the squash and stir, and then add the stock and the cinnamon or nutmeg.

2 Bring to the boil and simmer until all the vegetables are cooked – approx. 15 minutes. Purée the soup in a blender until smooth and then return it to the saucepan. Reheat gently, check the seasoning and serve with a spoonful of cream or buttermilk.

SHOPPING LIST
butternut squash
carrot
celery
cream or buttermilk (to serve)

OPTIONS

Serve with garlic bread or any bread of choice.

L: Replace the butter with 3 tbsp olive oil. Use buttermilk or crème fraiche in place of cream to serve, or serve without garnish.

G-F: Use a gluten-free stock. Omit the cinnamon powder unless sure it does not contain gluten. Alternatively, grind a small piece of cinnamon stick.

ASPARAGUS & LEMON SOUP

I first tasted this soup in Cyprus. The Greeks and Cypriots make many versions of *avgolemono* or lemon soup, using various vegetables and meats. It is tangy and delicious.

INGREDIENTS

15g butter

250g asparagus, washed

1 medium onion, finely chopped

1 leek, washed and cut into 1cm rounds

500ml (2½ cups) strong vegetable stock

juice of half a lemon

1 egg, beaten

¾ tbsp cornflour

100ml (½ cup) of milk

salt and white pepper to season

SHOPPING LIST

asparagus

leek

METHOD

1 The ends of asparagus are woody and tough. You can find where the woody part begins by bending the spear close to the end until it breaks off naturally at the beginning of this part. Do this with all the asparagus spears but keep the tough end pieces for flavouring the soup. Cut the top parts of the asparagus into 2cm pieces.

2 Heat butter in a saucepan, and gently sauté the onion until softened. Add the stock and the end pieces of the asparagus. Simmer gently for about 20 minutes. Remove the pieces of asparagus and discard.

3 Add the leeks and simmer gently for 5 minutes. Add the asparagus and simmer for a further 5 minutes.

4 Meanwhile whisk the egg and the lemon juice together. Mix the cornflour with the milk.

5 When the asparagus is tender, mix the egg and lemon juice with the cornflour and milk, and add to the soup. Check the seasoning and serve.

OPTIONS

The Cypriots have this with a little cooked white rice, or it can be served with bread or rolls.

L: Replace the tbsp butter with a tbsp olive oil. Use low-fat milk.

G-F: Make sure the stock used is gluten-free.

61217252ᵴ.

MUSHROOM & LEEK SOUP

If I had to choose the easiest, most delicious gourmet-type soup ever, this would be the one.

INGREDIENTS

100g butter

4 leeks, trimmed, washed and finely sliced

900g mushrooms, cleaned and chopped

½ glass of white wine

800ml (4 cups) strong chicken or vegetable stock

sliced scallions or chives to serve (optional)

SHOPPING LIST

leeks

mushrooms

scallions or chives, if using

METHOD

1 Heat the butter in a large saucepan over a medium heat, until it foams. Add the leeks and cook for about 5 minutes, without browning, until they begin to soften.

2 Turn up the heat a little and add the mushrooms. Fry on a medium to high heat for 5-7 minutes until the liquid from the mushrooms has evaporated and they are just beginning to turn brown.

3 Add the wine and cook on high for a minute before adding the stock. Bring to the boil and simmer for another couple of minutes. Serve with a sprinkling of scallions.

OPTIONS

Serve with rolls or bread of your choice.

L: Use 3 tbsp oil in place of the butter.

C-F: Omit the wine and, if children don't like 'bits' in their soup, liquidise.

G-F: Use gluten-free stock.

CELERY & STILTON SOUP

This is a universal favourite and can be a complete meal in itself. The amount of Stilton can be varied to taste, adding more to make a richer soup. The soup can be made in advance, without adding the cheese. In this case, reheat the soup slowly and add the cheese, just before serving.

INGREDIENTS

30g butter

5 medium-sized celery stalks, sliced in half lengthways and chopped into 1cm pieces

1 medium onion, chopped

1 clove of garlic, chopped

200ml (1 cup) milk

450ml (2½ cups) vegetable or chicken stock

½ tbsp cornflour, dissolved in 50ml (¼ cup) of milk

75g Stilton, crumbled (including the rind)

a little fresh parsley and crushed walnuts for serving (optional)

SHOPPING LIST

celery
Stilton
fresh parsley (to serve)
walnuts (to serve)

METHOD

1 Heat the butter in a saucepan and add the onion, celery and garlic. Cook gently, without browning, until the vegetables have softened a little.

2 Add the milk and stock and bring to the boil. Reduce the heat immediately and simmer until the vegetables are cooked. Liquidise – if you have a hand blender, this can be done in the saucepan, making sure you remove the pot from the heat before doing so.

3 Add the cornflour dissolved in milk, and cook until it thickens.

4 Just before serving, add the crumbled Stilton to the simmering soup and remove from the heat immediately. Stir until the Stilton has dissolved and serve immediately, garnished with parsley and a sprinkling of crushed walnuts.

OPTIONS

Serve with buttered crusty rolls or wholemeal bread.

L: Replace the butter with 1½ tbsp sunflower or corn oil and use low-fat milk.

C-F: Stilton may be a little strong for children – substitute with a mild Cheddar or some plain cream cheese.

G-F: Make sure the stock used is gluten-free.

FRESH TOMATO SOUP

This is good to make in the summer when there is a glut of tomatoes and they are cheap. Keep an eye out for price reductions on very ripe tomatoes that are nearing their sell-by date. You can also make and freeze the classic Tomato Sauce (see page 150) if you are batch buying ripe tomatoes.

INGREDIENTS

30g butter

1kg ripe tomatoes, chopped into 1cm cubes

2 large onions, chopped

2 carrots, diced

2 sticks of celery, sliced in half lengthways and chopped into 1cm lengths

1 tsp sugar

1 litre (5 cups) chicken or vegetable stock

1½ tbsp freshly chopped parsley

a little fresh cream or crème fraiche, to serve

salt and freshly ground black pepper

SHOPPING LIST

tomatoes, ripe
carrots
celery
fresh parsley
fresh cream, or crème fraiche (to serve)

METHOD

1 Heat the butter in a large saucepan and add the onions, carrots and celery. Cook until they soften but without browning – about 10 minutes.

2 Add the tomatoes, sugar and stock, cover and cook at a gentle simmer for about 30 minutes more. (It is important not to boil the tomatoes as this makes them bitter.)

3 Finally stir in the parsley and add a little black pepper. Check the seasoning and serve with a swirl of cream.

OPTIONS

Serve with garlic bread or toast. You can also add a tbsp boiled rice to each bowl just before serving.

L: Replace the butter with 2½ tbsp olive oil, leave out the sugar and replace the cream with a little low-fat crème fraiche.

C-F: Some children don't like 'bits' in their soup – in this case, liquidise.

G-F: Use gluten-free stock..

CREAM OF SPINACH SOUP

Spinach is a nutritious vegetable, high in antioxidants and minerals. For this recipe, it can be replaced by kale, radish tops or any similar green leaf.

INGREDIENTS

50g butter

450g fresh spinach (or about 300g frozen spinach, defrosted)

1 medium onion, chopped

1 clove of garlic, crushed

800ml (4 cups) chicken or vegetable stock

juice of half a lemon

a little grating of fresh nutmeg or a pinch of dried nutmeg

salt and freshly ground black pepper

150ml (¾ cup) fresh cream (to serve)

SHOPPING LIST

Fresh or frozen spinach
cream, fresh (to serve)

METHOD

1 Wash the fresh spinach in cold water until all traces of sand and soil have disappeared – depending on how clean the leaves are, this may take up to three washes. Chop into strips.

2 Melt the butter in a large saucepan until it begins to foam (but not change colour) and add the onion and garlic. Fry gently until the onion softens, then add the spinach. Stir fry for a minute before adding the stock, lemon juice and nutmeg. Bring to the boil and then reduce the heat to a simmer. Cover and continue simmering for about 10 minutes.

3 Purée the soup using a food processor or a blender. Return to the saucepan and reheat slowly. Taste the seasoning, adding salt and black pepper if necessary. Ladle into bowls and add about a tbsp of cream, swirling it around in the centre of the soup with a spoon.

OPTIONS

Serve with a lemon wedge, and crusty rolls or wholemeal bread and butter.

L: Use 2 tbsp olive oil instead of butter. Use low-fat milk in place of cream, to serve.

C-F: Some children may not like the taste of spinach, but soup can be a good way of getting them to enjoy it. Adding a splash of milk may help.

G-F: Make sure the stock used is gluten-free.

CARROT & POTATO HASH BROWNS

These are great for a starter or a light supper. Here I have seasoned them very simply with salt and black pepper but other seasonings are worth a twirl – curry powder, coriander, cumin, take your pick.

INGREDIENTS

300g (2 cups) raw potato, grated

300g (2 cups) raw carrot, grated

1 small onion, finely chopped

2 heaped tbsp chopped, fresh parsley

2 eggs, beaten lightly

2 tbsp sunflower or corn oil for frying

a generous knob of butter

salt and black pepper

To serve: 300ml (1½ cups) sour cream or yoghurt and chopped scallions or chives

SHOPPING LIST

carrot
fresh parsley
sour cream or yoghurt (to serve)
scallions or chives (to serve)

METHOD

1 Mix the carrot, potato and onion in a bowl. Squeeze the excess liquid out by hand and add the parsley and eggs. Season generously with salt and black pepper. Heat the oil in a pan until very hot but not smoking. Put a heaped tablespoonful of the mixture in the pan and flatten to a circle, about 1½ cm thick. Continue in this way until the pan is full., it makes around 8 hash browns.

2 Turn after a couple of minutes when golden underneath. Reduce the heat to medium, and cook for another eight minutes, turning occasionally, until golden on both sides.

3 Turn up the heat to maximum and add the butter to the pan. Turn the fritters so that both sides are coated lightly in butter.

4 Chop one whole scallion or the chives and add to the sour cream or yoghurt. Salt lightly and stir.

OPTIONS

Serve the fritters with the sour cream or yoghurt as a dip.

L: Use low-fat yoghurt or low-fat crème fraiche to serve.

G-F: Make sure that the sour cream or yoghurt you use does not contain gluten. If neither of these is available, use fresh cream and sour it with a squeeze of lemon juice or a little gluten-free vinegar – about a teaspoonful.

CITRUS SARDINE SALADS ON BLINIS

Tinned sardines can be quite strong, but the addition of lemon and onion make the overall effect light and tangy.

INGREDIENTS

1 120g tin of sardines in oil or brine, drained

juice and zest of 1 lemon

1 small onion, very finely chopped

1 tbsp of mayonnaise

4 blinis (small buckwheat pancakes) or 4 small rolls, halved and toasted (these can be lightly buttered or not)

rocket to serve (if unavailable, use shredded cos or any lettuce)

black or green olives to serve

salt and freshly ground black pepper

a little extra virgin olive oil (optional)

SHOPPING LIST

sardines in oil or brine
blinis, or rolls
rocket (to serve)
olives, black or green (to serve)

METHOD

1 Put the lemon zest and juice with the sardines into a food processor and blitz until shredded but not too smooth – leave a bit of texture. Remove any pieces of white lemon membrane that have not liquidised.

2 Put the sardines into a bowl and mix in the onion, mayonnaise and salt and pepper. Taste and check the seasoning. If it's too tangy, add a tsp of olive oil. Be careful here not to kill the taste of the sardines – the tanginess will be reduced by the blinis and lettuce.

3 Place a little rocket on each blini and cover with a little mound of the sardine mixture. Decorate with an olive or two, and serve immediately.

OPTIONS

Serve with a slice of lemon.

L: Use sardines in brine, a light mayonnaise and use thick slices of cucumber in place of the blinis.

G-F: If gluten-free blinis are not available, replace them with gluten-free bread.

PAN-SEARED AUBERGINE WITH MOZZARELLA

This recipe combines tastes of the Mediterranean with the complex flavour of the aubergine and the creaminess of the cheese, brought together by the garlic and a little sharp lemon.

Oven 190°C/375°F/gas mark 5

INGREDIENTS

1 large aubergine, washed but not peeled and cut into 8 slices, approx. ¾cm in width

2 cloves of garlic, crushed

4 tbsp extra virgin olive oil

1 mozzarella ball – about 125g drained weight – cut into 8 chunks.

1 lemon, quartered lengthways and, for serving, two of the quarters cut in half again

a little extra oil for the oven tray and the griddle pan

salt and freshly ground black pepper

SHOPPING LIST
aubergine
mozzarella ball

METHOD

1 Brush the oven tray and griddle pan with a little oil.

2 Brush the aubergine slices, on both sides, with half of the olive oil, and season with salt, black pepper and the juice of a quarter of the lemon.

3 Heat a heavy, ridged griddle pan until very hot (an ordinary, heavy pan will do but a ridged pan makes attractive lines on the aubergines as they cook). Fry the aubergine slices for about 3 minutes on each side until chargrilled and softened.

4 Mix the crushed garlic with the remaining olive oil, a little salt and pepper, and the juice of the remaining quarter of lemon.

5 Brush the fried aubergine slices with the garlic/oil mixture and place on the lightly oiled oven tray. Put a chunk of mozzarella on top of each aubergine slice and season with a little salt and freshly ground black pepper.

6 Bake for 15-20 minutes until the cheese turns golden. Serve immediately.

OPTIONS

Serve on their own, garnished with the remaining pieces of lemon.

L: Use low-fat mozzarella and reduce the oil to 2 tbsp.

C-F: If aubergine is a new taste for your children, then bringing an element of fun and involvement into its introduction often helps the process. I find that getting children to help in the making of food makes them more likely to like strange new tastes. This recipe could be finished off by children, allowing them to assemble the aubergine and cheese stacks, ready for the oven.

G-F: Use gluten-free mozzarella.

RED PEPPER CHICKEN BASKETS

These are really pretty and can be served hot or cold. The baskets can be made up to 2 days ahead and stored in an airtight container in the fridge. The filling can be made up to 3 hours ahead. You will need a muffin pan to bake the baskets.

Oven 170°C/340°F/gas mark 3½

INGREDIENTS

2 sheets of filo pastry, defrosted

40g butter, melted

I large red pepper, cut into Icm cubes

80g (½ cup) of cooked chicken, cut into Icm cubes

I tbsp cornflour

100ml (½ cup) cream

½ tsp mustard powder, mixed with I tbsp milk

I tbsp chopped fresh parsley

METHOD

I Brush pastry with melted butter and cut each strip into thin strips, approx. 5cm wide.

2 Criss-cross 4 strips in each muffin pan cup. Bake in the preheated oven for 5-7 minutes, until golden. If serving the starter cold, allow the baskets to cool and place in an airtight container in the fridge.

3 Cook the pepper in a little boiling salted water until tender. Drain and cool a little.

4 Put the pepper and chicken in a saucepan. Mix the cornflour and cream together and add to the saucepan. Bring to the boil, stirring constantly. Reduce the heat and continue to cook, still stirring, until the mixture thickens. Mix in the mustard and parsley.

5 If serving hot, spoon the chicken and pepper sauce into the baskets and serve immediately. If serving cold, allow the sauce to cool, refrigerate until needed and spoon the sauce into the cold baskets just before serving.

OPTIONS

These can be served alone, but a little fresh parsley or slivers of red pepper can be added for plate decoration.

L: Replace the tbsp of butter with a tbsp of corn or sunflower oil. Replace cream with half-fat crème fraiche.

SHOPPING LIST
filo pastry (freezer section)
red pepper
chicken
cream
fresh parsley

SHIOYAKI MACKEREL

Like sardines, mackerel is a fish that is both healthy and economical. This is a Japanese method – shioyaki – of cooking fish and meat. The fish or meat is covered in salt and left at room temperature for 15-45 minutes, then rinsed and grilled. It suits the flavour of mackerel particularly well. The fish is served with a sweet, soy-based sauce.

INGREDIENTS

2 whole mackerel filleted

a little oil for cooking

salt – preferably rock or sea salt

For the soy dip

150ml (⅔ cup) dark soy sauce

4cm fresh ginger root, chopped

4 tbsp sugar

To serve

1 medium carrot, grated

a little wasabi paste

METHOD

1 With a clean tweezers, remove any remaining bones from the fish fillets and cut off the tail piece. Rinse with cold water and pat dry. Salt very generously, until almost white, and leave for 15 minutes. Rinse well with cold water.

2 Heat the soy sauce, ginger and sugar in a pan, stirring well. Bring to the boil and simmer for 2 minutes. Strain.

3 Heat grill to high. Cover the grill pan with tinfoil and lightly oil. Place fish, skin side down on the grillpan and grill for 3-4 minutes until opaque. Remove from the heat, turn over, being careful not to break the fish, and gently scrape off the skin and any tail pieces, with a sharp knife.

OPTIONS

Serve with the soy dip, some shredded carrot and a little mound of wasabi about the size of a 5 cent piece. Plain boiled rice and/or salad goes well with this too.

L: Reduce the sugar to 2 tbsp.

C-F: Mackerel can be a strong fish for a child, but the sweetness of the soy-based sauce makes it a great recipe for introducing children to the fish. If can experiment by picking up the fish with chopsticks, and dipping it into the sauce before eating, the fish may be eaten up in a jiffy.

G-F: Check that the soy sauce is gluten-free.

SHOPPING LIST

mackerel fillets
dark soy sauce
carrot (to serve)
ginger root
wasabi paste or horseradish sauce (to serve)

Note: *Wasabi paste is available in Asian shops. It is a herb root that tastes like horseradish and is very hot. It adds greatly to the taste experience and also to the appearance of the dish, as its natural colour is pale green. It's sold in powder and paste form. However if it's not available, a little horseradish sauce can be used instead.*

STUFFED GARLIC MUSHROOMS

The large, mature mushrooms used in this recipe remind me of the field mushrooms I picked as a child. They would appear magically, overnight, after late-summer rain. We used to bring them home and put them on the top of the range to cook, just adding a little salt. The tops slowly filled up with delicious salty juice and the trick was to eat them without spilling any of the precious juice.

Oven 190°C/375°F/gas mark 5

INGREDIENTS

25g butter at room temperature

4 large mushrooms

1 medium onion, finely chopped

1 clove of garlic, crushed

1 tbsp lemon juice

1 tbsp chopped fresh parsley

salt and freshly ground black pepper

a little oil or butter for the oven tray

SHOPPING LIST

mushrooms, large
fresh parsley

METHOD

1 Wipe or brush the mushrooms clean – do not wash them as this will make them soggy. Carefully remove the stalks and chop them for use in the stuffing. Brush the tops of the mushrooms with lemon juice.

2 Put the onion, garlic, parsley and chopped mushroom stalks into a bowl and season liberally with salt and black pepper. Mix in the butter and taste to check the seasoning.

3 Grease the oven tray and place the mushrooms on it. Divide the stuffing between the mushrooms and bake for 30-40 minutes until golden brown on top.

OPTIONS

The mushrooms will be lovely and juicy, so crusty bread is perfect for mopping up the juices.

L: Replace the butter with 2 tbsp olive oil.

C-F: Set aside a mushroom or mushrooms for children and reduce the quantity of garlic by half on these.

THAI LOBSTER SALAD

Lobster is always a treat and when I get it on offer, which does happen from time to time, I love to make this salad. See note on page 232 on how to shell a lobster.

INGREDIENTS

4 whole, cooked lobsters, approx. 500g each, fresh or frozen

8 large leaves of iceberg lettuce, washed, dried and shredded

½ large cucumber, thinly sliced

juice of 1 lime

1 tsp sugar

1cm fresh ginger root, crushed

1 clove of garlic, crushed

1½ tbsp soy sauce

½ tbsp freshly chopped coriander

1 small red onion, sliced

1 tbsp oil

METHOD

1 If the lobster is frozen, defrost according to the instructions on the packet.

2 Heat the soy sauce, ginger and sugar in a pan, stirring well. Bring to the boil and simmer for 2 minutes. Strain.

3 Remove the lobster flesh from the shell and cut into small pieces.

4 Mix the rest of the ingredients, except the lettuce, together, with the lobster

5 Arrange the shredded lettuce on a plate and spoon the lobster salad on top.

OPTIONS

Serve with crusty rolls or toast.

C-F: Reduce the ginger and garlic by half and leave out the coriander.

G-F: Make sure the soy sauce is gluten-free.

SHOPPING LIST

lobster
iceberg lettuce
cucumber
lime
ginger root
fresh coriander
red onion

PANCETTA FRUTADA

The inspiration for this starter goes back to my London days and my Columbian friend Martha Elena. Plantain and bacon are a typical combination of flavours in Columbia. When experimenting with the ingredients for this dish I didn't manage to find plantain, so I've used regular banana instead.

Oven 220°C/425°F/gas mark 7

INGREDIENTS

1-2 firm bananas, a little under-ripe is better

2 large, firm pears

6 rashers of bacon

juice of half a lemon

a small knob of butter, melted

2 tbsp mayonnaise

16 small lettuce leaves, washed and dried

salt and freshly ground black pepper

SHOPPING LIST

bananas, a little under-ripe
pears, firm
bacon
lettuce

METHOD

1 Put the lemon juice into a shallow dish and season with salt and black pepper.

2 Slice each of the rashers into two strips, lengthways.

3 To assemble the frutada, core and quarter the pears, leaving the skin on. Dip the pears in the lemon juice and wrap a strip of bacon around each one.

4 Peel the bananas and cut into four pieces the same length as the pear quarters. Dip them in the lemon juice and wrap them in the remaining strips of bacon.

5 Grease an oven tray with half the butter and place the banana and pear frutada on it. Brush the bacon on the outsides with the rest of the butter and cook the frutada in the preheated oven for 20 minutes.

6 Heat the grill to maximum and grill the frutada for a couple of minutes, until golden brown.

7 Mix 2 tsp lemon juice with the mayonnaise until smooth. Arrange the lettuce on four plates and divide the frutada between them. Drizzle the mayonnaise over and serve.

OPTIONS

Serve with crusty rolls or buttered toast.

L: Trim the bacon of any fat and use low-fat mayonnaise.

C-F: These are not strong tasting but they may be an unusual taste for children – as an introduction, getting them to wrap up their own fruit in bacon should get them interested in eating the end result.

G-F: Some bacon contains gluten so ingredients should be read carefully to ensure your bacon is gluten-free.

SHREWD
EXPRESS

One of the lessons I have learned about food preparation is that it does not necessarily have to be time-consuming to be good. We live in a very busy world and for many of us, myself included, a meal is often something that needs to be thrown together at the end of a working day, when there is no time or energy for fussiness. I love my food and I like cooking but, on a daily basis, I don't want to spend hours in the kitchen. What is needed is something quick and simple that is, nonetheless, a treat for the taste buds. The recipes in this section all meet that requirement and are also fast and easy to cook if you have unexpected guests.

CHICKEN & SAUSAGE BAKE

This is fast and easy – just put all the ingredients together in an oven dish, mix them up with your hands and put it into the oven. Hey presto – dinner!

Oven 210°C/410°F/gas mark 6½

INGREDIENTS

8 chicken drumsticks or oyster thighs

450-500g sausages, chopped in half

6-8 good-sized potatoes, peeled and halved

1 large tomato, quartered

3-4 cloves of garlic, crushed

3-4 tbsp olive oil

1 tbsp chopped fresh parsley

salt and black pepper

SHOPPING LIST

chicken drumsticks or oyster thighs
sausages
fresh parsley

METHOD

1 Mix all the ingredients together in an oven dish with your hands until fully coated.

2 Bake on high for 30 minutes, then reduce temperature to 190°C/375°F/gas mark 5, baste and bake for another 45 minutes or until golden brown and the chicken is cooked through.

OPTIONS

This goes with most vegetables, or with a salad.

L: Use four chicken breast fillets, chopped into 6cm squares, and omit the potatoes.

G-F: Use gluten-free sausages.

MOZZARELLA CHICKEN

This chicken dish takes about 10 minutes from fridge to oven. It can also be prepared a few hours in advance and stored in the fridge in an oven dish covered with cling film. Then just pop it in the oven about 45 minutes before you're ready to eat, and prepare the vegetables and potato or rice as it cooks.

Oven 195°C/395°F/gas mark 6

INGREDIENTS

4 chicken breast fillets

1 mozzarella ball, 125g net weight

1 medium tomato, chopped

1 medium onion, chopped

1 tbsp grated Parmesan

a knob of butter for the chicken

salt and black pepper

a little oil to coat the oven dish

SHOPPING LIST

chicken

mozzarella ball

METHOD

1 Oil an oven dish large enough to take the chicken flat, and place the chicken in the dish. Season with the salt and black pepper, and smear with the butter.

2 Place in the preheated oven for 25 minutes.

3 Mix tomato and onion together, season with salt and pepper. Slice the mozzarella thinly.

4 When the 25 minutes are up, remove the chicken from the oven. Sprinkle half the tomato and onion over the breasts and cover with the slices of mozzarella. Season with salt and freshly ground black pepper. Sprinkle the remainder of the tomato and onion over the mozzarella and top with the grated Parmesan.

5 Return to the oven for 20 minutes, until the cheese is bubbling and the chicken is cooked through.

OPTIONS

Serve with mashed potato and vegetables or with boiled rice, drizzling the sauce over the rice.

L: Use low-fat mozzarella and serve with a plain salad instead of potato or rice.

G-F: Some mozzarella and Parmesan cheeses contain gluten – check the label. If you cannot find gluten-free cheese, substitute with a medium Cheddar.

GRILLED SALMON FILLETS

Easy, fast and they taste divine! The trick here, and indeed with most fish, is not to be tempted to overcook them.

Set grill at hot

INGREDIENTS

4 salmon fillets, about 170-200g each, approx. 2.5cm thick

25g butter or 1 tbsp olive oil

½ tbsp chopped fresh parsley

juice of half a lemon

salt and black pepper

SHOPPING LIST

salmon fillets
fresh parsley

METHOD

1 Wash and pat dry the salmon fillets. Feel for any stray bones and remove them with a tweezers. Spread some lightly oiled tinfoil on an oven tray and place the fillets skin side down on the foil. Rub with the butter or oil. Sprinkle the chopped parsley over them and drizzle the lemon juice on top. Grind a little black pepper over each fillet and place under the hot grill about 10cm away from the heat.

2 Grill for 7-9 minutes until the flesh flakes easily with a fork and is just starting to separate from the skin. If in doubt, remove from the heat and let stand for a few minutes before serving, as the salmon will continue to cook after being removed from the heat.

OPTIONS

Serve with steamed or boiled vegetables such as green beans, broccoli and new potatoes.

L: Use olive oil instead of butter and serve without potatoes.

C-F: It's especially important with children to ensure that all fish bones have been removed.

PORK CHOPS IN PAPRIKA SAUCE

This is naughty but oh so nice. So good was the sauce that I ran my finger around the pan afterwards to get the last of it!

INGREDIENTS

4 pork chops

2 tsp paprika

200ml (1 cup) cream

250ml (2 glasses) white wine

28g butter

1 tbsp oil of your choice

salt and black pepper

SHOPPING LIST

pork chops

cream

METHOD

1 Mix the paprika, salt and a good grinding of black pepper with the pork chops.

2 Heat the oil to a medium heat. Add the butter and fry the chops for approx. 5 minutes each side, until golden brown and cooked through. Remove to a warmed plate and cover.

3 Add the white wine to the pan and stir. Remove from the heat and stir in the cream being careful not to boil. Heat gently and serve over the chops.

OPTIONS

Serve with new potatoes and vegetables of your choice.

L: Trim the pork chops of any fat, use low-fat crème fraiche instead of cream and omit the butter.

G-F: Ensure that the paprika is gluten-free.

CHINESE CHICKEN BROTH

This is an adaptation of a favourite Chinese soup from a cheap yet wonderful London restaurant I used to frequent. In my version, I have replaced the meatballs of the original recipe, which are time-consuming to prepare, with chicken breast fillets. It is very simple, fast and totally delectable. It can be served as a starter or a main course simply by varying the amount of chicken used. Here, I have cut the chicken into chunks, which is more suitable for a main course. If you are serving it as a starter, use only one chicken breast, cut it into very thin strips, and serve the broth without rice.

INGREDIENTS

4 chicken breast fillets, cut into 2cm wide strips

1.2 litres (6 cups) strong chicken stock

ginger root, 3cm peeled and crushed

20g fresh coriander including stalks, washed and lightly chopped

2 pak choi

4 scallions, washed and chopped diagonally into 1cm pieces

METHOD

1 Bring stock to the boil in a saucepan. Stir in the ginger and half of the coriander and cook for half a minute.

2 Add the chicken and simmer for about 10 minutes until the chicken is cooked through.

3 Add the pak choi and the rest of the coriander and cook for about half a minute. Add the scallions just before you serve.

SHOPPING LIST

chicken breasts
ginger root
fresh coriander
pak choi
scallions

OPTIONS

Serve by itself or add a little boiled rice.

G-F: Check that the stock does not contain gluten.

SHRIMP CHILLI FRY

Rina, a friend from Goa, worked with me for a while in Dubai and she introduced me to chilli fries. This is my shrimp chilli fry and when I make it I think of Goa, with the long, pale-coloured sandy beaches, the palm trees and, of course, the sunshine. I've never actually been – but one can dream!

INGREDIENTS

600g shrimps or prawns, precooked (if frozen, defrost completely as per instructions)

1-2 green chillies, finely chopped

2 large onions, thinly sliced

4 medium-sized tomatoes, chopped

2 tbsp sunflower or corn oil

2-3 tbsp vinegar – to taste

salt

SHOPPING LIST

shrimps or prawns, precooked

METHOD

1 Heat the oil and fry the onions until golden. Add the chillies (I use only one. Goans, who like their food very hot, would probably use 3-4), tomatoes and a little salt, and sauté gently for a few minutes.

2 Add the shrimps and cook for a minute or two.

3 Then add the vinegar and cook gently for a few more minutes until the sauce reduces.

4 Check the seasoning and serve.

OPTIONS

Serve with plain boiled rice, or naan or pitta bread.

L: Use only 1 tbsp oil and squid instead of prawns, as the former is much lower in fat.

G-F: Check that the vinegar you use is gluten-free.

LAMB CUTLETS WITH LIME & CORIANDER DRESSING

The dressing is the knock-out thing here. It can be poured over a variety of meat and fish, and it goes really well with lamb cutlets.

INGREDIENTS

8 lamb cutlets

For the dressing

juice of 3 limes

15g fresh coriander (including stems)

2 cloves of garlic

3 tbsp peanut, sunflower or corn oil

1 red or green chilli

1 dessertspoon sugar

1 tbsp fish sauce

SHOPPING LIST

lamb cutlets

limes

fresh coriander

fish sauce

METHOD

1 Blitz all the dressing ingredients in a food processor until finely chopped. Stir until the sugar dissolves.

2 Coat the lamb chops with half the dressing and marinate for about 30 minutes, while you prepare the accompaniments.

3 Grill, fry or barbecue the lamb chops for 3-4 minutes on each side, depending on how well done you like them.

4 Plate the cutlets, drizzle with the remainder of the dressing and serve immediately.

OPTIONS

Serve with a fresh green or mixed salad and new potatoes. Also good with stir-fried vegetables and plain boiled rice.

L: Trim the meat of all fat. Use olive oil for the dressing.

C-F: Prepare the cutlets to the end of Stage 3 and serve the children's portions without additional dressing.

G-F: Ensure the fish sauce is gluten-free.

CABBAGE CURRY

I got this recipe from Dammika, my Sri Lankan friend, and this dish is extremely popular in her country. As it's fast, easy and delicious, one can understand why.

INGREDIENTS

1 small cabbage (or half a large cabbage), washed, dried and shredded

1 large onion, sliced

1 tbsp sunflower oil

1 tsp curry powder or 8-10 fresh curry leaves

¾ tsp mustard powder

½ tsp turmeric

1½ tsp salt

300ml (¾ can) coconut milk

40ml (¼ cup) water

SHOPPING LIST

cabbage
curry leaves (optional)
coconut milk

Note: *Leftover coconut milk can be added to smoothies and curries, or add a little sugar and have on porridge. In cake recipes, half the milk can be replaced with coconut milk.*

METHOD

1 Mix cabbage, curry powder or leaves, mustard, turmeric and salt in a bowl.

2 Heat oil in a saucepan and stir fry the onion for a few minutes until golden. Add cabbage and spice mixture and water, reduce the heat and stir fry for a couple of minutes.

3 Cover with a lid and cook gently for 5 minutes.

4 Increase the heat and add the coconut milk. Bring to a simmer and simmer for 2-3 minutes until the cabbage is cooked but still has texture.

OPTIONS

Serve with boiled rice, either on its own or as an accompaniment to other curries.

L: Use low-fat coconut milk.

C-F: Reduce the spices by half.

G-F: Check that the curry powder (if not using leaves), mustard and turmeric are gluten-free.

GARDEN PEA SALAD

This is a simple and quick salad, and the nuts calm the dressing nicely. It is also lovely and light, as well as being very healthy.

INGREDIENTS

450g (3 cups) frozen peas

1 large onion, chopped finely

40g (⅓ cup) mixed chopped nuts

2½ tbsp sunflower oil or olive oil

2 tbsp vinegar

1½ tsp mustard powder

1½ tbsp honey

salt and black pepper

METHOD

1 Cook peas in boiling water for one minute less than it says on the packet. Drain and rinse with cold water.

2 Make the dressing by shaking the mustard, sunflower or olive oil, vinegar, honey and salt and pepper together in a lidded jar (a cleaned, used jam jar is perfect for this).

3 Put all the ingredients into a bowl and mix together. Adjust the seasoning if necessary, and serve.

SHOPPING LIST

frozen peas
mixed, chopped nuts
honey

OPTIONS

This can be served as a starter, a side dish or a main course. Great with wholemeal bread and/or new potatoes.

L: Use olive oil and use nuts like almonds, hazelnuts, pistachios and walnuts, which are lower in saturated fats, than brazils, pine nuts and cashews.

C-F: Ensure nuts are chopped up small.

G-F: Check that the vinegar and mustard are gluten-free.

BROCCOLI SALAD

I had this salad at a barbeque at Lesley and John Sullivan's place. Lesley is not taking all the credit herself but says she got the recipe from her sister Trish when living in Capetown. It is yummy! It is also very easy to make. I prefer it a little less sweet, so I have reduced the sugar content.

INGREDIENTS

For the dressing

200ml (1 cup) mayonnaise

50g (¼ cup) sugar

2 tbsp white vinegar

For the salad

350g broccoli, raw and cut into bite-size chunks

1 medium onion, finely chopped

75g (½ cup) raisins

8 bacon rashers, fried on a low heat until crisp

SHOPPING LIST

broccoli

raisins

bacon rashers

METHOD

1 Wash broccoli and chop into bite-sized chunks.

2 Fry rashers until crisp and, when cooled a little, cut into slivers.

3 Combine the dressing ingredients. Mix salad ingredients together and add the dressing.

4 Refrigerate for a couple of hours before serving, to allow the flavours to blend.

OPTIONS

Add a few cashews and serve with crusty bread or bread of choice.

L: Use light mayonnaise and do not add cashews.

C-F: Cut the broccoli into small pieces. If your children don't like broccoli, try telling them that they are giants and broccoli spears are little people's trees that giants eat – it worked for both my son and my nephew!

G-F: Use gluten-free mayonnaise, vinegar and bacon.

YOGHURT CHICKEN

This is a Greek-inspired recipe – it's about as healthy a list of ingredients as you can get and it tastes very, very good. If the budget stretches to it, the dried herbs could be replaced with fresh ones. Marinate overnight if time permits but it can also be popped straight into the oven as soon as it's prepared.

Oven 170°C/340°F/gas mark 3½

INGREDIENTS

4 chicken breast fillets

400ml (2 cups) natural yoghurt

4 cloves of garlic, crushed

juice and zest of 1 lemon

1 tsp mixed dried herbs

½ tsp dried thyme

salt and freshly ground black pepper

SHOPPING LIST

chicken, breasts or oyster thighs or drumsticks
natural yoghurt

METHOD

1 Slice the chicken breasts in half lengthways so that you have eight thin pieces of chicken breast about 1cm thick – this will mean they cook faster and will be less likely to dry out.

2 Put the chicken into a bowl, and mix with all the other ingredients. If time permits, refrigerate for a couple of hours or preferably overnight. (To reduce washing up, marinate the chicken in a large Pyrex or ceramic oven dish, and put it straight into the oven to cook.)

3 Cook for 35-40 minutes, until the chicken is cooked through. While it is cooking, prepare the vegetables or salad to go with it.

OPTIONS

Serve with boiled potatoes and vegetables of your choice or a simple Greek salad.

L: Use low-fat yoghurt.

C-F: Serve with a little less of the sauce for children.

G-F: Some yoghurts contain gluten – always check the label.

CHEDDAR BEEF & PEPPERS

This is beef with a lovely colourful, crunchy pepper-and-cheese topping.

Oven 200°C/400°F/gas mark 6

INGREDIENTS

500g lean beef mince

1 large onion, finely chopped

1 clove of garlic, finely chopped

3 small peppers (or ½ of three large peppers) of different colours

100g medium or mature Cheddar, grated

1 tsp paprika

½ tsp mixed spice

½ tsp dried oregano

1 tbsp oil of your choice

salt and freshly ground black pepper

SHOPPING LIST

beef mince
peppers, different colours
Cheddar, medium or mature

METHOD

1 In a shallow ovenproof dish, heat the oil until hot but not smoking. Add the onions and stir. Lower the heat to medium and cook the onions gently, without browning, until soft – about 5 minutes.

2 Turn the heat up to maximum and add the mince, stirring to separate. Once the meat has browned, add the garlic, spices and oregano, and stir well. Check the seasoning and place in the preheated oven. Bake until the mince is cooked – about 15 minutes.

3 Meanwhile wash the peppers, remove the white centres and chop into pieces about 1cm square.

4 Sprinkle the peppers over the beef and then sprinkle the Cheddar over the peppers. Season the top with salt and freshly ground black pepper and return the dish to the oven. Cook until the cheese is bubbly and golden – about 5 minutes.

OPTIONS

Serve with baked potatoes or pitta bread. This also goes really well with tacos or tortillas and salad.

L: Use low-fat cheese.

C-F: Reduce the spices by half.

G-F: Ensure spices are gluten-free.

SHREWD
EUROPEAN

This section includes traditional Irish, English and French recipes and some from further afield in Europe. I lived in the Greek part of Cyprus for a few years and loved the cuisine, so there is a fairly strong Greek influence too. The recipes are made either from ingredients that are generally reasonable in price or ingredients that are frequently on special offer. To save time, I often cook for two days and freeze the extra or keep if in the fridge for later in the week. Some of the recipes in this section, such as lasagne, moussaka, lamb stew and fasulia lend themselves particularly well to this.

COTTAGE PIE

This great everyday meal is a favourite with all ages but especially with children. Putting the vegetables in with the mince is a good way to get the younger folk to eat them. You can speed this recipe up by adding 600g of frozen mixed vegetables instead of the fresh carrots and frozen peas.

Grill: Preheat to hot

INGREDIENTS

500-550g beef mince

2 medium to large onions, chopped

1 tbsp oil of your choice

2-3 medium carrots, washed and cut into 1½cm cubes

300g (2 cups) frozen peas

50ml (¼ cup) strong beef stock

1 level tbsp cornflour or flour, dissolved in 100ml (½ cup) warm water

8-10 medium to large potatoes, peeled, washed and halved

100ml (½ cup) milk

a knob of butter plus a little for dotting the top of the pie

freshly ground black pepper

SHOPPING LIST
beef mince
carrots
frozen peas

METHOD

1 Heat oil in a saucepan and stir fry the onions until light gold in colour. Add the mince and cook on high, stirring to separate. Add the beef stock and stir. Reduce the heat, cover, and cook very gently for about 20 minutes.

2 Bring about 3cm water to the boil in a saucepan, add the carrot and bring to the boil. Add the peas and bring to the boil again. Strain, leaving a little water back and add to the mince. Cook gently together for 5 minutes. Stir in the cornflour and water mixture and bring back to the boil, stirring all the while.

3 Reduce the heat and simmer for a few minutes until the cornflour thickens the sauce. Check the seasoning, adding salt and freshly ground black pepper if necessary. Remove from the heat, cover and set aside.

4 Meanwhile add the halved potatoes to a large saucepan of water and bring to the boil. Reduce the heat and cook until tender, approx. 15 minutes.

5 Drain and return to a low heat. Add the milk and bring to a simmer. Add the knob of butter and seasoning, and mash well.

6 Put the mince/vegetable mixture into an oven dish and dot with the mashed potatoes. Spread the potato over the mince, covering it completely and score with a fork. Dot with a little butter and place under a hot grill until golden on top.

OPTIONS

This is a complete dish on its own, or you can serve with extra vegetables, such as broccoli, green beans or corn.

L: Use extra lean mince and low-fat milk and do not thicken with cornflour. Do not add any butter to the potatoes when mashing.

G-F: Make sure the stock used is gluten-free.

CLASSIC LASAGNE

Not only is this a great 'comfort' dish but it's also ideal for a gang. I have a great big oven dish that I use when making lasagne, which serves about twelve, and I freeze two-thirds for later use.

Oven 180°C/350°F/gas mark 4

Oven dish 30cm x 20cm x 5cm deep, approx.

Serves 6

INGREDIENTS

500g lean beef mince

2 medium onions, chopped

2-3 cloves of garlic, peeled and chopped

1 tbsp oil

1 tin of chopped tomatoes

1 tsp dried mixed herbs

½ tsp dried thyme

1 tbsp freshly chopped parsley

2 tbsp tomato purée

salt and freshly ground black pepper

12 sheets of lasagne pasta

For the white sauce

40g butter

3 tbsp flour or cornflour

600ml milk

salt and a little white pepper

a little butter or grated Parmesan for the top

METHOD

1 Heat the oil in a large pan or saucepan, and add the onions. Cook, without browning, until the onions begin to soften and add the garlic. Cook together for a couple of minutes and add the mince. Stir to separate the mince and cook over a medium heat until browed.

2 Push the meat to the side and add the tinned tomatoes, the herbs and salt and black pepper. Heat these, without boiling, and mix in the meat and onions. Cover and simmer for 30 minutes. Remove from the heat and stir in the tomato purée.

3 Meanwhile cook the lasagne in boiling salted water, to which a little oil has been added, until al dente. Drain, rinse well in cold water and drain again.

4 To make the white sauce, melt the butter in a saucepan, over a low to medium heat, and stir in the flour. Cook gently, without browning for a couple of minutes, stirring all the time. Then add about a third of the milk and whisk thoroughly. Turn up the heat a little and continue whisking until the sauce thickens. Then add the rest of the milk, and continue to whisk until the sauce thickens – about 5 minutes. Season with salt and white pepper. Cover and set aside.

5 In the oven dish, place one-third of the meat and cover with four lasagne sheets. Repeat the process twice and then pour the white sauce over the top.

6 Bake in the oven for about 10 minutes until the top has become firm and then brush with a little melted butter or sprinkle with a little grated Parmesan.

7 Bake for about another 20-30 minutes until it's golden on top. Serve immediately.

OPTIONS

Serve with crusty rolls, garlic bread or salad of your choice. I love chips or sautéed potatoes with lasagne, but this is really upping the fat and calorie content. Follow with several brisk turns around the block!

L: Use olive oil for lower cholesterol, leave out the mozzarella and use low-fat milk for the white sauce.

G-F: Use gluten-free lasagne. Ensure Parmesan is gluten-free.

SHOPPING LIST
beef mince
lasagne sheets
fresh parsley
tinned tomatoes

MOUSSAKA

Moussaka is one of the best-known Greek dishes, with layers of aubergine and meat, topped with béchamel sauce. When aubergines are in season and prices are low, it is quite a reasonably priced dish, but it does take quite a bit of time to make. I often make it over two days, cooking the meat and aubergine part first and preparing the potato (if using) and béchamel the next day. I often make one and a half times this amount and freeze the remainder in two containers.

Oven 230°C/450°F/gas mark 8

Oven dish 30cm x 20cm x 5cm deep

Serves 6

INGREDIENTS

500g lean minced beef

2 large aubergines

1 large onion, chopped finely

3 tbsp oil of your choice

1 large, ripe tomato, chopped

1 tbsp tomato purée

5-6 medium potatoes

100ml (½ cup) hot chicken stock

½ tsp dried thyme

½ tsp dried basil

½ tsp mixed herbs

salt and freshly ground black pepper

For the béchamel sauce

60g butter

60g flour or cornflour

500ml milk

1 egg

salt and white pepper

SHOPPING LIST

mince
aubergines

METHOD

1 Peel the aubergines and put them in a bowl of salted water – about 1 tbsp salt to 1½ litres of water – for 30 minutes.

2 Heat one tbsp of oil in a pan and fry the onions, without browning, until they soften and become a little transparent. Add the meat, and stir until it is separated and has changed colour. Stir in the tomato and cook for a minute or two. Then add the hot stock and herbs and check the seasoning. Bring to a simmer and cook gently for 30 minutes.

3 Remove the aubergines from the salted water and dry with kitchen paper. Lightly brush with 1 tbsp oil and place in a single layer on an oven tray. Bake in the preheated oven for 30 minutes until they are beginning to brown lightly. Mash

them into the meat mixture with the tomato purée, and check the seasoning adding salt and black pepper if necessary.

4 Reduce the oven temperature to 180°C/350°F/gas mark 4.

5 Peel the potatoes and cut them into 1cm thick slices. Wash the slices in cold water and dry with kitchen paper. Heat the remaining tbsp of oil in a frying pan and lightly brown the slices of potato.

6 Put half of the meat mixture in the oven dish, add a layer of potato and then the rest of the meat. Put the rest of the potatoes on top and set aside while you make the béchamel.

7 Heat the butter in a saucepan until it begins to foam. Add the flour or cornflour and stir vigorously using a whisk. Cook for a minute and then add about a third of the milk. Whisk until sauce thickens and then add the rest of the milk, whisking until it comes to the boil. Whisk in the egg, reduce the heat to the lowest setting and simmer gently, still whisking, for 1 minute. Season with salt and white pepper and pour over the meat and potato mixture.

8 Place in the preheated oven and bake for 10 minutes. Remove and dot with a little butter. Put the dish back in the oven and bake until it is golden brown on top – about 35-40 minutes.

OPTIONS

Serve with boiled rice and/or Middle Eastern Salad (see page 144). If you haven't included potato, or even if you have, it's very nice with chips or sautéed potatoes. It's great with green vegetables such as broccoli or spinach or lightly fried courgette slices. Some toasted pitta or garlic bread would be good too.

L: Omit the potatoes and use low-fat stock and low-fat milk.

C-F: Although it contains aubergines, which some children may not like, they melt into the meat and herbs and do not feature prominently in the finished dish, which should make it palatable to kids.

G-F: Make sure stock used is gluten-free.

MARINATED ROAST CHICKEN

Chicken is a great low-fat meat, as well as being a good value buy, and here we marinate it beforehand for extra taste and juiciness. It's a lovely, garlicky, lemony marinade and, if you can, baste it regularly instead of covering it with foil. It makes for a more intense taste and a crispier skin. If that seems like a chore, put on some music, pour yourself a glass of your favourite tipple (purists would say it should be something like an earthy Cote Rotie from the northern Rhone, but I would say drink whatever does it for you) and then, basting with the juices from the roasting pan every 15-20 minutes won't seem such a chore.

Oven 230°C/450°F/gas mark 8

INGREDIENTS

1 chicken, 1.5kg in weight

1 onion, sliced

6-8 medium to large potatoes

2 tbsp oil of your choice

For the marinade

3-4 large cloves of garlic, crushed

grated rind and juice of half a lemon

2 tbsp olive oil

¾ tsp salt and
plenty of black pepper

SHOPPING LIST

1 chicken

METHOD

1 Mix the marinade ingredients together and smear over the cleaned chicken. Refrigerate overnight or for 24 hours if possible.

2 Put 1 tbsp oil in a roasting pan with the marinade, add the chicken and place in the preheated oven for 30 minutes, basting after 15 minutes.

3 Meanwhile peel the potatoes and cut into half. Rinse with cold water and pat dry with kitchen paper. Season them with salt and black pepper and rub with 1 tbsp oil.

4 Baste the chicken and add the potatoes and onions to the pan. Return to the oven and reduce the heat to 220°C/425°F/gas mark 7. Cook for about another hour, basting every 15 minutes. To check if cooked, insert a knife between the thigh joint and the body of the bird – juices that come out should be clear, not pink.

OPTIONS

Serve with whatever vegetables you like, or with a Greek or Arabic salad. If you wish to make a gravy, pour off any oil or fat from the roasting dish and add a little chicken stock – about 200ml and 1 tsp flour or cornflour. Place this on the hob, stir until it thickens. Continue cooking for a couple of minutes, stirring all the while. Check the seasoning, adding salt and black pepper if necessary.

L: Use olive oil and roast the chicken without potatoes. Serve with a salad and simple steamed or boiled vegetables.

Note: *This dish can be made with the same weight of chicken pieces too – drumsticks, thighs or breasts, or a mixture of these – whatever is on offer. In this case, reduce the cooking time to 45-60 minutes, checking that the meet is cooked through and there are no pink bits.*

CHICKEN & RED PEPPER PASTA

This a great way to use leftover chicken. It gets its wonderful flavour from the red peppers and the mustard. Add some fresh cream and it gets even better.

INGREDIENTS

650g (4 cups) cooked chicken

4 large red peppers

2 tsp cornflour

500ml (2½ cups) cream

2 tsp French mustard

2 tbsp fresh, chopped flat leaf parsley

400g dried pasta

SHOPPING LIST

cooked chicken
red peppers
cream
French mustard
fresh flat leaf parsley

METHOD

1 Chop the chicken into 1cm squares.

2 Cook the pasta in a large saucepan of boiling water until al dente. Drain, but leave a little of the cooking water in the pasta.

3 Heat about 2cm of well-salted water in a saucepan until boiling. Add the chopped peppers and simmer until cooked but still firm – this will take about 5 minutes. Drain and add in the chicken.

4 Dissolve the cornflour and the mustard with a little of the cream and add in the rest of the cream. Add to the chicken and simmer until the sauce thickens.

5 Add the chopped parsley and serve with the pasta.

OPTIONS

If preferred, this dish can be served with boiled rice or potatoes instead of pasta.

L: Use breast meat and replace the cream with the equivalent amount of low-fat crème fraiche.

C-F: Make as above but reduce the mustard and the cream by half. Set aside the children's portion and add extra cream and mustard to the adult portion, to taste.

G-F: Use gluten-free cornflour and pasta. If the mustard is not gluten-free, replace with 2 tsp of English mustard powder, mixed with a tsp of gluten-free vinegar.

BARBEQUED LEMON & HERB CHICKEN

The Cypriot menu is varied and always interesting, and eating with friends is an important feature of Cypriot life. I was lucky enough to live there for a number of years, and this is one of the ways we prepared chicken for a barbeque. I cannot overemphasise the benefits of marinating meat. Not only does the flavour improve, but the marinade tenderises the meat.

INGREDIENTS

1kg chicken pieces (a mix of leg and breast pieces is good for the flavour and juiciness)

100ml (½ cup) oil

2 cloves of garlic, crushed

2 tbsp lemon juice

1 tbsp honey

1 tbsp dried oregano

½ tbsp dried rosemary

salt and black pepper

METHOD

1 Combine all the ingredients, except the chicken, in a large bowl. Add the chicken and mix well, until it is covered completely with the marinade.

2 Refrigerate and leave for at least 2 hours, stirring a few times. Ideally, leave overnight in the fridge.

3 Grill on medium hot coals for 35-40 minutes, turning to ensure it doesn't burn, until all the chicken pieces are cooked through.

SHOPPING LIST

chicken pieces or a whole chicken, jointed

honey

OPTIONS

Serve with any or all of the following: a fresh salad, baked potatoes, natural yoghurt.

L: Use chicken breasts on the bone only and skin them. Replace the oil with 1 tbsp olive oil.

GRILLED WHITING WITH LEMON BUTTER

Whiting offers great value and has a very delicate taste. This recipe is very simple and light. Whiting is in season for most of the year, but is at its best in the winter months.

INGREDIENTS

4 whiting fillets

juice of ½ lemon

30g butter

1 tbsp fresh chopped parsley

salt and black pepper

SHOPPING LIST

whiting fillets

fresh parsley

OPTIONS

Serve with new potatoes and steamed green vegetables.

L: Replace the butter with 1 tbsp olive oil.

METHOD

1 Check the fillets for any remaining bones and remove them with tweezers. Wash the fish in cold water and pat dry with kitchen paper. Season thoroughly with salt and black pepper.

2 Heat the grill to maximum.

3 Heat the butter in a large, shallow frying pan and add the fillets, skin side up. Cook gently for half a minute and turn. Place the pan under the heated grill, about 2cm from the heat, and cook for about 4 or 5 minutes until fish turns white and is cooked through. Do not overcook or it will become dry.

4 Carefully remove the fillets from the pan, using two spatulas if necessary. Put the pan back on the heated cooker top, add the lemon and parsley and stir to mix with the cooked butter. Pour the lemon sauce over the fish and serve immediately.

TUNA PASTA

There must be a thousand versions of tuna pasta and most of them are easy, fast, tasty and good value to make. This one has an Italian influence and can be served hot or cold.

INGREDIENTS

2 tins of tuna in oil – approx. 200g each

1 medium onion, chopped

2 stalks of celery, chopped

2 medium tomatoes, chopped

3 cloves of garlic, chopped

1 tbsp capers, chopped finely

¼ glass white wine

400g dried pasta

salt and freshly ground black pepper

SHOPPING LIST

tinned tuna, in oil

celery

capers

OPTIONS

Serve with crusty bread.

L: Add the oil from one of the cans of tuna and discard the other.

C-F: Replace the wine with the equivalent of vegetable stock.

G-F: Use a gluten-free pasta.

METHOD

1 Squeeze the oil from the tins of tuna into a saucepan (without the tuna) and heat. Add the onion, garlic and celery and cook for about 5 minutes.

2 Then add the chopped tomatoes, the capers and a little salt and cook gently, uncovered and without boiling, for about 20 minutes, until the vegetables have softened.

3 Break the tuna into chunks and add to the pot with the wine. Stir together and simmer for a further 5 minutes. Check the seasoning, adding salt and freshly ground black pepper if necessary.

4 Meanwhile cook the pasta in a large pot of boiling, salted water until al dente. Strain, but leave a little of the cooking liquid in the pasta.

5 Serve the sauce over the pasta or serve mixed together.

COD & PEPPER KEBABS

Cod is a fish that is very often on special offer, but this dish can be made with other, similar, white fish so keep your eye out for what's on offer. Alternatives that work are haddock, coley, hake and whiting. This is a light and very healthy dish, which is full of flavour. It is easy to make and cooks in a jiffy. Don't be tempted to leave the fish and vegetables in the marinade for longer than about 15 minutes, as the acid in the marinade will start to cook the fish and it will become mushy.

INGREDIENTS

500g cod fillets

2 peppers of different colours, washed and deseeded

1 large onion, peeled

2 cloves of garlic, crushed

3 tbsp olive oil

juice of 1 large lemon

¾ tsp ground or 1 tbsp fresh coriander

1 tsp salt

a little black pepper

9 or 10 wooden skewers, soaked in water for 30 minutes

SHOPPING LIST
cod fillets
peppers, different colours
fresh coriander (if using)
wooden skewers

METHOD

1 Remove any bones left in the cod with a tweezers and then remove the skin. Cut into chunks about 2-3cm square.

2 Cut the peppers and the onion into chunks 2-3cm in size.

3 In a large ceramic or plastic bowl, mix together the garlic, olive oil, lemon juice, coriander, salt and black pepper. Add the fish, the peppers and the onion. Mix well, cover and refrigerate for 15 minutes.

4 Heat the grill to high.

5 Remove the fish, onion and peppers from the fridge and thread onto the skewers. Place on a grillpan, which has been covered with lightly oiled foil, and put under the hot grill, about 2cm from the heat.

6 Grill for about 8 minutes, until the fish is cooked through, turning a couple of times to ensure even cooking.

OPTIONS

Serve with boiled rice or buttered new potatoes.

Note: *The marinade for this cod is also delicious with chicken, pork, beef or lamb. Meat, unlike fish which will become mushy, benefits from being left in the marinade for a few hours or even overnight. This allows the flavours to penetrate the meet and the acid in the marinade to tenderise it.*

FISH PIE

This is the fish equivalent of cottage pie: tasty, economical comfort food. The list of ingredients seems a little long but, trust me, it's not difficult to make. It's best eaten fresh.

A mixture of seafood such as cod, prawns and salmon is perfect – some supermarkets do a ready-to-use fresh fish pie mix, which can be very reasonably priced. I usually buy fish when it's on special offer and freeze it in small portions, so that it can be used with other fish for recipes such as this or for one-person meals.

The topping can be potato or puff pastry. If you use pastry, make sure you seal the sides well or the pie will dry out.

Oven 190°C/375°F/gas mark 5

Oven dish 30cm x 20cm x 5cm deep

INGREDIENTS

500g mixed fish, cut into small squares (about 1½cm – leave small prawns whole)

70g mushrooms, chopped

1 medium onion, chopped

1 carrot, chopped

1 stick of celery, chopped

1 tbsp freshly chopped parsley

1 bay leaf, dried or fresh

a couple of sprigs of thyme or ¼ tsp of dried thyme

¾ glass of white wine

100 ml (½ cup) water

½ tbsp flour or cornflour, mixed with 50ml (¼ cup) milk

butter for the potatoes and the oven dish

50ml (¼ cup) fresh cream

6-8 medium potatoes, cooked and mashed, or 250g puff pastry, for the top

a little milk for the potatoes and for the top of the pastry, if using pastry

salt and white pepper

SHOPPING LIST

mixed fish, fresh or frozen
mushrooms
carrot
celery
fresh parsley
puff pastry
fresh cream, if using

METHOD

1 Put the onion, carrot, celery, herbs (except parsley), water and wine in a saucepan and cover. Bring to the boil, reduce the heat and simmer for about 10 minutes until the vegetables are almost cooked.

2 Add the uncooked fish and bring to the boil. Remove the fish from the saucepan and scrape off the skin. Allow to cool. Check for bones and remove any found.

3 Add the flour or cornflour mixture to the saucepan and bring to the boil, stirring all the time until the mixture thickens. Then boil vigorously until the liquid reduces to a thick sauce – you need just enough liquid to cover the vegetables. Cool a little and check the seasoning.

4 Add the fish, cream, mushrooms and parsley.

5 Put the fish and sauce mixture into the buttered oven dish.

6 Meanwhile, cook the potatoes till tender and mash with a little milk and butter. Season with salt and pepper and spread over the fish mixture. This is easier to do if you spoon blobs of potato here and there over the fish, and join up the blobs using a fork. Smooth the top with a knife and then use the fork to make a pattern on the potato. Dot with butter and bake in the preheated oven for about 30 minutes, until golden on top.

7 If using pastry, roll it out a little bigger than the top of the pie dish, and place on top of the fish, making sure the edges are sealed well. Brush with a little milk and bake as above.

OPTIONS

Serve immediately with any of the following – leeks, broccoli, carrots, mangetout, green beans.

L: Use low-fat milk instead of ordinary milk and cream and, if using potatoes, reduce the quantity by a third to make a thinner topping.

C-F: Ensure that all bones are removed before serving fish to children.

G-F: Use cornflour instead of flour and check that the cornflour is gluten-free.

LAMB STEW

For me, lamb stew is about lots of herbs and onions, and very, very tender lamb. I like to put the vegetables in towards the end as I like them to retain more texture but you can add the vegetables at the beginning if you wish.

INGREDIENTS

1kg gigot lamb chops

1 large onion, sliced

1 leek, washed and cut into 2cm rounds

4-6 cloves of garlic, chopped

2 tbsp fresh parsley, chopped

a few sprigs of fresh thyme or ½ tsp dried thyme

4-5 large carrots, peeled and cut into thirds

5-6 large potatoes, peeled

1 chicken or vegetable stock cube

salt and black pepper

SHOPPING LIST

gigot lamb chops

leek

fresh parsley

fresh thyme

carrots

METHOD

1 Cut the lamb into large chunks (or, better still, get this done at the meat counter), retaining the bone. Remove any fat and gristle.

2 Put the meat, onion, leek, herbs, garlic and stock cube into a large saucepan and cover with water. Season with salt and pepper and bring to the boil. Cover and simmer gently until the lamb is very tender, usually around 3 hours. If you have a pressure cooker, this will take only around 35-45 minutes. Remove the bone and any remaining fat and skin.

3 Add the carrots and bring to the boil, then add the potatoes and bring to the boil again.

4 Reduce the heat and simmer until the vegetables are cooked, about 30 minutes. Adjust the seasoning and serve.

OPTIONS

Serve with crusty bread.

L: Trim the chops of all fat.

G-F: Ensure the stock is gluten-free.

GREEK FRICASSEE OF LAMB

This is a very common Greek dish and one of my favourites. If you have never tried it before, don't be put off by the idea of adding lettuce to a lamb stew – it's different but it really is delicious. Shoulder of lamb is both great value and particularly flavoursome.

INGREDIENTS

500g cubed lamb shoulder

2 tbsp good quality olive oil

1 bunch of scallions, chopped

1 medium onion, sliced

1 tbsp freshly chopped parsley

100ml (½ cup) hot chicken or vegetable stock

1 large cos lettuce, cut into strips about 2cm wide

juice of 1 lemon

1 egg, beaten

100ml (½ cup) milk

1 tsp of cornflour

salt and freshly ground black pepper

SHOPPING LIST

cubed lamb shoulder or leg

scallions

fresh parsley

cos lettuce

METHOD

1 Heat the oil in a large saucepan and add the lamb, scallions, onions, parsley and salt and pepper. Fry all together for about 5 minutes. Add the hot stock and the lettuce. Cover and simmer gently until the lamb is cooked – about an hour.

2 Meanwhile mix the milk and cornflour together. Slowly beat the lemon juice into the beaten egg.

3 Remove the meat from the heat. Whisk the milk and cornflour, and the egg and lemon juice together and stir into the meat. Leave for about a minute and serve.

OPTIONS

Serve with boiled rice or boiled potatoes.

L: Trim the lamb of all fat. Leave out the milk and cornflour.

C-F: Make to Stage 2. Remove the child portion(s) and complete the recipe as above. Children may not like the lettuce in the sauce – if so, serve meat and sauce only.

G-F: Check that the stock and cornflour are gluten-free.

FASULIA

This is a dish of meat and beans. I have eaten many variations of this, which is very common in Greece, Cyprus, Turkey and the Levant. This one is very simple and one that I cook regularly.

INGREDIENTS

500g cubed lamb, shoulder is ideal, but stewing lamb of any kind is fine

300ml (1½ cups) hot vegetable or chicken stock

350-400g (2-3) cups of frozen green beans

2 medium onions, chopped

1 large, ripe tomato, chopped

4 cloves of garlic, 2 chopped, 2 crushed

1 tbsp oil

1½ tsp mixed spice

2 tbsp tomato purée

25g fresh coriander, chopped (it must be fresh, not dried)

juice of ½ a lemon

½ tbsp butter

salt and freshly ground black pepper

METHOD

1 Heat the oil in a saucepan and fry the meat, onions and chopped garlic together for about 5 minutes, until the meat is sealed but not browned.

2 Add the stock, tomato, spice and salt and black pepper and simmer together until the meat is tender. How long that takes depends on the quality of the meat. If it's shoulder and tender, it could take as little as 30 minutes, but if the meat is tough, it could up to 3 hours. If it's cooking for a long time, add more stock if necessary.

3 Boil the green beans according to the instructions on the packet, until tender. Add to the meat, with the tomato purée and stir. Heat gently, without boiling.

4 Heat the butter in a pan and add the crushed garlic. Fry for a few minutes until golden and then add the chopped coriander and fry for another few minutes until the coriander dries out a little. Add the lemon and a couple of spoonfuls of the meat stock to the pan, mix it with the garlic and coriander and pour the mixture into the meat and beans.

5 Simmer together for about 5 minutes and serve.

OPTIONS

Serve with boiled rice and/or hot pitta bread

L: Trim the meat of all fat. Replace the butter with olive oil.

C-F: Make as far as the end of Stage 3. Remove the child portion(s) and complete the recipe as above, reducing the garlic, coriander, lemon and butter to taste.

G-F: Make sure the stock and mixed spice are gluten-free.

SHOPPING LIST
lamb shoulder or any stewing lamb
frozen green beans
fresh coriander

KLEFTICO

I think the Greeks do roast lamb better than anyone else. This is my version of this famous dish, marinated with wine and aromatic vegetables and then slow-roasted in the oven. Leg of lamb is often on special offer later in the year so watch out for it, and remember, you can always bulk buy and deep freeze.

Oven 230°C/450°F/gas mark 8

INGREDIENTS

2-2½kg leg of lamb on the bone

1 glass dry white wine

2 tbsp olive oil

2 bay leaves

2 tsp dried oregano

2 carrots, halved

2 sticks of celery, chopped into quarters

2 leeks, trimmed, washed and halved

2 onions, quartered

4 cloves of garlic, cut into slivers

1 unwaxed lemon, quartered

500g potatoes, cut into quarters

salt and freshly ground black pepper

SHOPPING LIST

leg of lamb on the bone

carrots

celery

leeks

unwaxed lemon

METHOD

1 Cut the meat into 4 or 5 big pieces, leaving the bone piece in. Put all the ingredients in a large casserole. Stir and marinate in the fridge for 2-3 hours, stirring again halfway through.

2 Discard half the marinade liquid and cover the casserole with a lid. Place the casserole in the hot oven for 15 minutes.

3 Reduce the oven temperature to 120°C/340°F/gas mark 4, and cook for another 4-5 hours, until the meat is so tender that it is almost falling off the bone.

4 Allow to rest for 5-10 minutes before serving.

OPTIONS

Remove the meat from the bone and break it up into small chunks. Serve with the potatoes and vegetables. Pitta bread and natural yoghurt go very well with this dish.

L: Trim the meat of all fat and omit the potatoes.

G-F: If using stock, make sure it's gluten-free.

BACON & CABBAGE

The seeds of my passion for good food were sown with my mother's cooking. Like many Irish women of her time, her repertoire of savoury dishes was not particularly extensive, and mainly Irish. However, she was very precise about those things that she did cook, and her food was very tasty. She made the best bacon and cabbage I have ever tasted. When cooked properly, this classic Irish recipe is delicious and soul-enriching, especially on a rainy night! A pressure cooker is great for speeding up the cooking of the bacon.

INGREDIENTS

1kg collar bacon

1 vegetable stock cube

1 small green cabbage

a little butter

SHOPPING LIST

collar bacon

green cabbage

METHOD

1 Put the bacon in a saucepan and cover with cold water. Leave overnight and drain.

2 Cover with fresh, cold water and bring to the boil. Add the stock cube. Simmer for 50 minutes per kilo and 30 minutes extra at the end. Remove from stock, rest for 5 minutes and carve into thin slices. (Note: The bacon, after soaking, can be cooked in a pressure cooker for about 30 minutes and then complete the recipe as per the instructions below.)

3 While the bacon is cooking, prepare the cabbage. Remove the outer leaves of the cabbage and discard. Wash and cut the remaining cabbage into thin slices. Add to the bacon 20 minutes before it finishes cooking.

4 When the bacon is cooked, remove it from the saucepan and rest it for 5 minutes in a warm place before carving it into slices.

5 Drain the cabbage and season with salt, pepper and a little butter.

OPTIONS

Serve with parsley sauce and boiled potatoes.

L: Omit the butter and serve with extra vegetables instead of potatoes.

G-F: Ensure the bacon and stock used are gluten-free.

MUSHROOM-STUFFED PORK FILLET

Pork fillet can be stuffed in a variety of ways. Here the mushrooms and apple stuffing complements the meat perfectly.

Oven 190°C/375°F/gas mark 5

INGREDIENTS

1 pork steak 800g-1kg, trimmed of fat and gristle

1 large onion, chopped finely

250g mushrooms, cleaned and chopped

½ cooking apple, preferably a Bramley, chopped

2 tbsp olive oil

1 tbsp butter

salt and black pepper

3-4 cocktail sticks or kitchen string to secure meat

SHOPPING LIST

pork steak
mushrooms
cooking apple, preferably a Bramley
string, if using

METHOD

1 Heat oil and butter in a pan over a medium heat. Add the mushrooms, onion and apple and cook until soft. Season with salt and pepper and set aside. If you are not going to stuff the pork and put it into the oven immediately, leave the stuffing to cool.

2 Lightly oil an oven tray and put it into the oven.

3 Cut the pork in half lengthways, but not all the way through – leave about 1cm. Flatten out and beat with a pestle or the flat of your hand until it's about 1cm thick. Season with salt.

4 Place the cooked mushroom stuffing on the pork and secure with the string or cocktail sticks. Place on the heated oven tray in the oven, and roast until cooked through – 50-60 minutes.

5 Remove from the oven and cover with foil. Allow to rest for 15 minutes, remove the cocktail sticks or string and then cut into slices about 2cm thick. Serve immediately.

OPTIONS

Serve with white wine sauce, parsley mash and green vegetables.

L: Omit the butter.

TURKEY & RED PEPPERS

Tired of turkey curry after Christmas? Well, here's a tasty alternative. The sweetness of the peppers and the tang of the soured cream make a delicious contrast. Enjoy!

INGREDIENTS

500g cooked turkey, diced (small dice, about 1½cm square)

3 red peppers, washed, and cut into 1cm squares

1 large onion, chopped

2 large, ripe tomatoes, washed and chopped

1 chicken or vegetable stock cube, dissolved in 50ml (¼ cup) boiling water

400ml (2 cups) fresh or soured cream

1 tbsp oil

large knob butter (don't stint here!)

SHOPPING LIST

cooked turkey
red peppers
cream, fresh or sour, as preferred

METHOD

1 Heat oil and butter in a saucepan. Cook the onion gently until it softens – about 10 minutes.

2 Add the tomatoes, and the stock and bring to a simmer.

3 Place the turkey on top, without stirring, and the peppers on top of the turkey, reduce temperature and cook at a very low heat until the turkey is heated through thoroughly, and the peppers have softened a little.

4 Add the cream and stir well. Season and serve.

OPTIONS

Serve with buttered, boiled rice or mashed potatoes, or with toasted pancetta.

L: Use low-fat crème fraiche instead of fresh or soured cream. Leave out the butter altogether.

C-F: Make as far as the end of Stage 3. Remove child portion(s) and then add cream to taste

G-F: Ensure a gluten-free stock is used. If using sour cream, ensure it's gluten-free. If a gluten-free sour cream is not available, add a tsp of lemon juice or vinegar to fresh cream to sour it.

PORK CHOPS WITH ANCHOVIES

Pork chops marinated in a delicious paste of garlic and anchovies, slightly sweetened and piquant. The pork can be replaced with sliced pork loin or chicken breast fillets if preferred.

INGREDIENTS

4 loin pork chops about 1½cm thick, bone in or boneless (bone is less inclined to be dry, but the marinade will help keep the chops moist)

1 tin of anchovy fillets in oil, approx. 30g net weight

3-4 cloves of garlic

1 tbsp oil

½ tsp sugar

2 tbsp cider vinegar

salt and freshly ground black pepper

SHOPPING LIST

pork chops
anchovy fillets in oil

METHOD

1 Drain the anchovies and keep the oil aside. Grind them with the garlic, sugar and ½ tsp salt. I use a pestle and mortar for this. When they are ground into a paste mix in the oil from the anchovy tin.

2 Put the chops into a bowl and smear with the garlic and anchovy paste, and leave for about 30 minutes to marinate.

3 Heat the oven on the lowest setting and put the dinner plates in to warm.

4 Heat the oil in a pan until hot but not smoking. Remove the chops from the bowl, scraping the marinade paste off the chops back into the bowl as you do so. Keep the marinade aside. Place the chops in the hot pan and sear on each side for one minute. Reduce the heat a little and continue cooking the chops for another 6-8 minutes until cooked through. Remove to the warmed plates.

5 Add the garlic and anchovy paste to the hot pan and stir fry for about a minute until slightly golden. To make the gravy, pour in the vinegar and stir it in for about a minute, without letting it evaporate. Pour the gravy over the chops and serve immediately.

OPTIONS

Serve with stir-fried vegetables or boiled cabbage and boiled potatoes.

L: Trim the chops of any fat, reduce the oil to ½ tbsp and the sugar to ¼ tsp.

C-F: The combination of anchovies and garlic may not appeal to children. Simply cook their chops without any marinade and reduce the marinade for the remaining chop(s) to taste.

G-F: Check that the cider vinegar does not contain gluten.

POULET À L'ORANGE

Don't be put off by the seeming long list of ingredients, as this is quite an easy dish as well as being great value. The floured chicken is browned, the onions and bacon are sautéed together and added to the chicken with all the rest of the ingredients, and then the whole thing is baked in the oven for about 40 minutes. It has a delicious tangy sweet and sour sauce.

Oven 210°C/410°F/gas mark 6½

INGREDIENTS

1 chicken, approx 1.5kg, jointed and skinned

1 tbsp flour or cornflour, seasoned with salt and black pepper

1 medium onion, chopped

2-3 rashers of bacon, chopped into 1cm squares

250ml (1¼ cups) hot chicken stock

juice of 1 large orange

1 large clove of garlic, chopped

1 tbsp vinegar, ideally cider vinegar

1 tbsp oil

a knob of butter (about 10g)

1 tsp brown sugar

¾ tsp dried, mixed herbs

salt and freshly ground black pepper

METHOD

1 Put the seasoned flour or cornflour into a bowl. Toss the chicken in the flour to coat it.

2 Heat the oil and butter in a flameproof casserole or heavy ovenproof saucepan and sauté the onions and bacon until the onions are golden. Remove and set aside.

3 Add the chicken to the pan and fry until slightly golden. Return the onions and bacon to the pan and add the hot stock. Then add all the other ingredients and stir. Bring to the boil, stirring until the sauce thickens.

4 Cover and place in the preheated oven. Bake for about 40 minutes until the chicken is cooked through, stirring after 20 minutes. Check the seasoning and serve.

I love French food. The variety is endless – from the seafood and charcuterie of the north to the quiches and preserves of the east; Burgundy casseroles such as boeuf bourguignon and coq au vin; cassoulet, piperade and bouillabaisse in the south – and of course wine from all regions. I have included more of my favourite French recipes in the Shrewd Vegetarian, Shrewd Entertaining and Shrewd Dessert chapters of the book.

OPTIONS

Serve with buttered rice and mangetout or green beans.

L: Leave out the butter and reduce the flour or cornflour to a 1/2 tbsp. Use halved chicken breasts in place of whole chicken.

G-F: Check that the cornflour, bacon, stock and vinegar are gluten-free.

SHOPPING LIST
chicken
rashers of bacon
orange

SHREWD
ASIAN

Here in Ireland, there has been a surge of interest in Asian food in recent years. One can understand why, as there is a wealth of diverse and rich cuisines to choose from. These are some of my own favourite recipes that embody the shrewd ethos: cheap, delicious and fun to make. Asian cuisine is known for its distinctive flavours and this section includes food from the Middle East – with its aromatic spices and subtle tones – spicy curries from Inida, and some easy but mouth-watering dishes from China.

KOFTA

Kofta is a type of meatloaf found in the Middle East and Asia. It's a delicious mixture of meat, spices and herbs that is very versatile. This recipe is a Middle-Eastern version. It can be rolled into balls and cooked with yoghurt, or barbecued on skewers. Here we will cook it on a tray in the oven with potatoes and tomatoes.

Oven 220°C/425°F/gas mark 7

INGREDIENTS

For the kofta

450-500g lean beef mince

1½ tsp mixed spice

½ tsp dried mint

½ tsp freshly ground black pepper

½ tsp salt

1 large white onion

3 cloves of garlic, peeled

approx. 20g flat leaf parsley

Other ingredients

5 or 6 medium potatoes peeled and sliced ½cm thick

1 tin chopped tomatoes

100ml (½ cup) hot water

salt and freshly ground black pepper

sunflower or corn oil for frying

METHOD

1 If you have a food processor, blitz the onions and garlic for 30 seconds on medium and stir. Blitz for another 30 seconds. Add parsley (including stalks) and blitz until finely chopped. Alternatively chop onion, parsley and garlic very finely with a knife. Add this to the mince with the mint, spice, salt and some black pepper and mix thoroughly with your hands.

2 Place mixture into a lightly oiled oven dish, pat it down to 2cm thick and put in the preheated oven for 10 minutes.

3 Peel and slice potatoes and deep fry or shallow fry in hot oil until golden on each side. Drain on kitchen paper and sprinkle lightly with salt.

4 Heat chopped tomatoes gently in a saucepan until hot but make sure not to boil them. Add a little salt and hot water.

5 After 10 minutes, remove the mince from the oven. Layer the potatoes over the mince and cover with the tomato mixture. Return to the oven, turn the heat down to 200°C/400°F/gas mark 6 and cook, uncovered, for 40 minutes.

Note: This is the recession-proof version, if you have a bit of lolly to spare, drop the dried herbs, increase the fresh parsley to 30g, and add 1 tbsp fresh mint. Fresh, ripe tomatoes can be substituted for canned.

OPTIONS

Serve with any or all of the following:

boiled rice; plain yoghurt; pitta bread; baguette/French stick.

L: Use extra-lean mince and serve without the potatoes.

C-F: Reduce the mixed spice to ¾ tsp.

G-F: Make sure that the mixed spice is gluten-free.

SHOPPING LIST
lean mince beef
flat leaf parsley
tinned chopped tomatoes

MINCE & GREEN PEA CURRY

Adding vegetables to the mince stretches it further and makes for a more economical meal. In any case, in the West we have a tendency to eat too much meat and anything that reduces that in favour of more vegetables is good. Here the peas add a sweetness to the curry, which can be made mild or spicy by either leaving out the chilli or adding an extra one.

INGREDIENTS

500g lean beef or lamb mince

2 medium onions, finely chopped

6-8 cloves of garlic, peeled and finely chopped

1 chilli, very finely chopped

2cm root ginger, finely chopped

2½ heaped tsp of a good quality hot Madras curry powder

100ml (½ cup) of vegetable stock

300g (2 cups) green peas – I use frozen

2 tbsp tomato paste

2 tbsp oil

METHOD

Heat the oil in a saucepan, add the onions, garlic, ginger and chilli, and cook gently until the onions have softened. Add the mince and the curry powder and cook, stirring, for a couple of minutes so that the mince does not stick together. Cook until the mince changes to a lighter colour, then add the stock. Bring to the boil and simmer until the meat is tender, about 15-20 minutes.

2 Meanwhile cook the peas in about 100ml of water until tender but still firm. Without draining them, add the tomato paste and heat through, making sure not to boil.

3 Add the peas and tomato to the mince and simmer gently together for about 10 minutes.

OPTIONS
Garnish with freshly chopped coriander and lemon quarters and serve with yoghurt and boiled basmati rice.

L: Use extra-lean beef mince and reduce the oil to 1 tbsp.

C-F: Reduce the spices by half and leave out the chilli altogether. The chilli can be sprinkled over the adult meal.

G-F: Ensure that the curry powder and stock are gluten-free.

SHOPPING LIST
mince (beef or lamb)
peas
chilli
root ginger

KIBBE

Lebanon is famous for its mezze, which is traditionally a meal of one hundred and one small, tempting dishes, which are continuously served as one eats. Stuffed kibbe balls are one of the dishes which feature regularly in this meal. This dish combines meat (lamb or beef) with bulgar (cracked) wheat and spices. The Lebanese, who consider kibbe to be their national dish, usually make it with lamb. It can be made into balls and fried in oil, or cooked on a tray in the oven. Sometimes it is stuffed with meat, onions and spices. The unstuffed version (kibbe nayeh) is often eaten raw, and there are varying opinions as to whether or not this is safe. This is a basic, cooked version and is very fast and easy to prepare.

Oven 180°C/350°F/gas mark 4

Oven dish 30cm x 20cm x 5cm deep, approx.

INGREDIENTS

500g beef mince

125g bulgar wheat

2 large onions, quartered

1½ tsp mixed spice

⅓ tsp each of salt and black pepper

½ tbsp oil

a little butter for the top

SHOPPING LIST

beef mince

bulgar wheat (available in the health food section of some supermarkets, in most health food shops and in some Asian shops)

METHOD

1 Place the bulgar in a bowl, cover with cold water, and soak for 30 minutes. Squeeze out the water and set aside.

2 Put the onion quarters in a food processor and process until pureed. Add the meat, the soaked bulgar and all the other ingredients except the butter and oil, and process together until smooth.

3 Oil the oven dish and press the kibbe on to the dish. Smooth out and score the top into squares or diamonds with a knife. Bake in the preheated oven for about 40 minutes until light gold on top.

4 Remove from the oven and lightly butter the top. Serve immediately.

Note: *Bulgar wheat is also a common ingredient in the food of many countries including the Levant, Mediterranean countries, and Iraq and Iran. Its high nutritional value makes it a good substitute for rice or couscous and it can also be added to soups and salads.*

OPTIONS

Serve with natural yoghurt or tsatsiki (a dip made with natural yogurt, cucumber, garlic and mint) and hot pitta bread, and a salad dressed with lemon and olive oil.

L: Serve with low-fat yoghurt or low-fat tsatsiki.

G-F: Replace the bulgar wheat with the same quantity of buckwheat.

BEEF CURRY

They say that the secret of a good curry is a lot of onion and a lot of oil. I would tend to go with the former and not go overboard on the oil. In this curry, which I make regularly, I substitute water for some of the oil, and use a good quality, ready-made curry powder, instead of individual spices, to speed up the process.

INGREDIENTS

500g sirloin steak, chopped into 2cm cubes (or 500g stewing steak)

2 large onions, thinly sliced

4 cloves of garlic, chopped

2 medium carrots, scraped and chopped into 4 parts

2 medium potatoes, quartered

1 medium tomato, chopped

1-2 green chillies, very finely chopped

3 tbsp sunflower or corn oil

3 heaped tsp of a good quality hot Madras curry powder

100ml (½ cup) boiling water

salt and freshly ground black pepper

SHOPPING LIST

sirloin steak

carrots

METHOD

1 Mix the beef with half the curry powder and ½ tsp salt. Cover and refrigerate for at least 2 hours and preferably overnight. Note: Cover tightly to prevent the smell of curry invading the fridge.

2 Mix the potatoes and carrots with the remainder of the curry powder and ¼ tsp salt.

3 Heat half the oil in a saucepan and add half the chopped onions. Fry until light gold in colour – about 5 minutes. Add the chopped chilli and half the garlic and stir fry for one minute. Add the carrot and potato and stir well before adding the boiling water. Cover, reduce the heat and simmer until the vegetables are cooked – about 15 minutes.

4 Meanwhile heat the remainder of the oil in a frying pan until hot. Add the beef to the pan and sear on all sides. Push the beef to one side and stir in the remainder of the onion and garlic and the chopped tomato. Stir fry for one minute before mixing it in with the beef.

5 Add the hot, cooked carrot and potato mix and cover. Reduce the heat and simmer until the meat is cooked through – about 5 minutes. Serve hot.

STEWING BEEF VERSION

1 Replace the sirloin steak with the same weight of stewing beef. Cook the meat as above until the tomatoes have been added. Add 70ml (⅓ cup) of boiling water and cover. Reduce the heat and simmer gently until the meat is tender, stirring occasionally. Depending on the toughness of the meat, this can take up to 3 hours. If it starts to dry out before the meat is tender, add a little more water. The water should be almost gone by the end of the cooking time.

2 Cook the vegetables as in Stages 2 and 3 above and add to the meat when it's cooked. Stir and simmer for 5 minutes and serve.

OPTIONS

Serve with any or all of the following: boiled basmati rice; plain yoghurt; tomato and onion salad; poppadoms (available in Asian markets ready to be fried).

L: Trim the meat of any fat. Reduce the oil to one tbsp and omit the potatoes.

C-F: Unless your children love curry, they may find this too spicy. In Asian countries a little curry is mixed with a lot of yoghurt and rice, when serving small children.

G-F: Use gluten-free curry powder. Poppadoms are usually made from lentil flour, sometimes with the addition of rice flour and hence are gluten-free, but always check the package.

> **Note:** For this recipe I've specified sirloin steak – which, if it's on special offer, can be great value. However, a perfectly good, better-value alternative is stewing steak, and I've included details for that method too – the only difference being that it takes longer.

BEEF WITH BLACK BEANS & GREEN PEPPER

This has been my favourite Chinese dish since my days living in London and is a great dish to make when you get steak on offer.

Serves 2

INGREDIENTS

Meat and marinade

250-300g good quality steak, preferably fillet or rump, cut into strips about 1cm wide and 3cm long

1 tbsp light soy sauce

1 tsp sugar

1 tbsp Chinese rice wine or dry sherry

½ tbsp toasted sesame oil

salt and white pepper

Other ingredients

4-5 cloves of garlic, peeled

1cm ginger root, peeled

3 tsp black beans

1 large onion, sliced

1 green pepper, sliced

2 tbsp sunflower, corn or peanut oil

1 tsp cornflour, mixed with 1 tbsp light soy sauce

METHOD

1 Put the meat and marinade ingredients into a bowl and refrigerate for at least an hour and preferably overnight.

2 Crush together the garlic and ginger and mash in the black beans. Add 1 tbsp of the oil.

3 Heat 1 tbsp of the oil in a seasoned wok (or frying pan) until it begins to smoke. Count to 20 seconds and add the meat. Leave for a minute without stirring and then stir fry for a couple of minutes more. Remove and keep warm.

4 Add the onion and green pepper to the wok, stir and cover. Cook for 2 minutes. Remove the cover and add the meat again along with the garlic/ginger/bean mixture and stir fry together for a further 2 minutes.

5 Turn off the heat, mix in the cornflour mixture and stir together until the sauce thickens. Serve immediately.

OPTIONS

Serve with boiled rice

L: Use lean steak and skip the cornflour. Reduce the cooking oil to 1 tbsp.

C-F: Chop up some pieces of beef very small and serve with rice and a very small amount of sauce.

G-F: Use gluten-free soy sauce, black beans and cornflour. If using sherry, check that it is gluten-free as some sherries have added caramel colouring which may contain gluten. Check too, that the sesame oil is free from additives which may contain gluten.

SHOPPING LIST

fillet or rump steak
Chinese rice wine or dry sherry (it's worth investing in a bottle of Chinese rice wine if you plan to cook Chinese food often)
toasted sesame oil (as with rice wine, this imparts its own unique flavour, and is good to have in the cupboard if you like to cook Chinese food)
ginger root
black beans
green pepper

Note: *The black beans might be a little difficult to find in the supermarket and a trip to an Asian market may be necessary. I buy the canned variety. Unused beans can be removed from the tin and frozen, and they are fine for at least a couple of months. To make life easy, I put handy, recipe-sized portions in small freezer bags and keep them all together in a Tupperware box, as the small bags can be hard to find in the freezer.*

This recipe is for two people, because an average wok or frying pan cannot accommodate a larger quantity, so if you are cooking for more, just double up on the ingredients and repeat the process.

SEBAANECH

'Sebanech' (seb aan ekh) is the Arabic word for spinach and this is a very common dish in the Mediterranean Arab areas. It can be made up in a large batch and frozen to keep for days when you are busy, or just don't feel like cooking. It's a gently spiced, meaty dish, lightened by the lemon and coriander.

INGREDIENTS

500g lean mince, beef or lamb

600g frozen spinach, preferably chopped

2 medium onions, chopped

2½ tbsp oil of your choice

a knob of butter

6 cloves of garlic, 3 chopped, 3 crushed

1 tsp ground coriander

¾ tsp mixed spice

25g fresh coriander, washed and chopped

juice of half a lemon

300ml (1½ cups) chicken stock

SHOPPING LIST

lean mince, beef for lamb
frozen spinach
fresh coriander

METHOD

1 Heat 1 tbsp oil in a saucepan and add one of the chopped onions. Fry gently for a few minutes, until it begins to turn transparent.

2 Turn up the heat a little and add the mince. Fry, stirring, for a few minutes until separated. Lower the heat and add the ground coriander, mixed spice and the chopped garlic. Cover with a lid and leave to cook gently for about 15 minutes, until tender.

3 Meanwhile heat 1 tbsp oil in a saucepan and fry the remaining onion gently. Add the stock and the spinach. Bring to the boil and cook gently for 5 minutes. Add to meat mixture and simmer together for 5 minutes.

4 Heat ½ tbsp oil in a frying pan. Add the butter and the crushed garlic, and cook for a few minutes until the garlic is cooked and beginning to turn gold at the edges. Add the fresh coriander and fry on a medium heat until the coriander darkens and is beginning to crisp. Pour over the lemon juice and add to the mince and spinach mixture.

5 Cook all together for 5 minutes more, season if necessary (salt will have been added with the stock cubes so be careful here) and serve.

OPTIONS

Serve with boiled rice and/or pitta bread.

L: Reduce the oil to one tbsp and omit the butter.

C-F: Make as far as Stage 3 and set aside the child portion(s). Complete the recipe as above, adding garlic, coriander and lemon juice to taste.

G-F: Make sure the mixed spice and stock are gluten-free.

CHICKEN SATAY

This is a Chinese version of pure comfort food. Don't be put off by the somewhat long list of ingredients, it's very fast and simple to prepare.

INGREDIENTS

Chicken and marinade

700g chicken oyster thighs, skinned, boned and cut into 5cm strips (the same quantity of chicken breasts can be substituted here)

3 cloves of garlic, finely chopped

2cm fresh ginger root, finely chopped

1 tbsp fish sauce

Sauce

1 tbsp sunflower, corn or peanut oil

1 large onion, finely chopped

2 cloves of garlic, finely chopped

2cm fresh ginger root, finely chopped

1-2 green or red chillies, finely chopped

2 heaped tbsp peanut butter

1 tin (400ml) coconut milk

1 tbsp light soy sauce

1 tbsp brown sugar

1½ tbsp fish sauce

juice of half a lime

10 wooden skewers, soaked for an hour in cold water

METHOD

1 Mix the chicken with the rest of the marinade ingredients and refrigerate for at least an hour.

2 Meanwhile, heat the oil in a saucepan and add the onion, garlic, ginger and chillies. Cook on a medium to high heat until the onion is golden, about 5 minutes.

3 Reduce the heat and add the rest of the ingredients. Simmer gently for about 10 minutes, stirring all the while. Remove from the heat and keep warm.

4 Preheat the grill to high.

5 Put chicken onto the skewers and grill on a lightly oiled grill pan for about 5 minutes each side, until no longer pink. (Remove a large piece of chicken from a skewer and cut through the thickest part to check it's cooked through.)

6 Put on heated plates, cover with the sauce and serve immediately.

OPTIONS

Serve with boiled rice.

L: Use chicken breast fillets instead of thighs and low-fat coconut milk.

G-F: Check that fish and soy sauces are gluten-free.

SHOPPING LIST

chicken, oyster thighs or breasts
ginger root
fish sauce
peanut butter
coconut milk
lime
wooden skewers

MAQLUBA

Maqluba is a Levantine dish, which Palestinians have made their own. The Arabic word 'maqluba' means upside down. The dish is cooked in a pot and then turned upside down onto a serving dish. The meat, vegetables and rice are cooked altogether in the same pot, allowing the flavours to mingle deliciously. It is usually made with aubergines, meat and rice but there are several variations, and this is a chicken and vegetable version.

INGREDIENTS

8 chicken pieces – dark meat is best for this recipe so oyster thighs or drumsticks would be suitable here. If preferred, the skin can be removed.

1 medium cauliflower, separated into large florets and washed

3-4 medium carrots, scraped, washed and cut into three

2 medium onions, peeled and chopped

510g (3 cups) basmati or other good quality long grain rice, washed and drained

2 tsp mixed spice

sunflower or corn oil for deep frying the cauliflower

salt and a little black pepper

SHOPPING LIST

chicken, drumsticks or oyster thighs, or breasts if making leaner option
cauliflower
carrots
lime
wooden skewers

METHOD

1 Put chicken, onions, spice, salt and pepper into a saucepan, add 900mls (4½ cups) of water and bring to the boil. Simmer for 15 minutes. Add the carrots, bring back to the boil and remove from the heat. Drain the stock into a heatproof jug or another pot and keep aside with the chicken and carrots.

2 Heat the oil and deep fry the cauliflower for two to three minutes until golden. Drain on kitchen paper.

3 In a large pot, with 2 handles that do not come up above the level of the top of the pot, add layers of carrots, chicken and cauliflower with the rice sprinkled in between each layer. It's important to put a layer of carrots at the bottom of the pot, because the sweetness in the carrots will caramelise them slightly, which adds to the flavour of the dish and looks good when the pot is turned upside down at the end.

4 Season the stock generously with salt – it has to include enough seasoning for the rice also. Add at least 800mls (4 cups) of the stock to the chicken mixture, adding water if necessary until covered.

5 Cover with a tightly fitting lid and bring to the boil. Reduce heat and simmer very gently for about 15 minutes. Turn off heat and leave on the warm cooker, without opening the lid, for another 15 minutes.

6 Remove the lid and put a large serving dish or tray, with sides, upside down on top of the pot. Grasping the handles of the pot and the serving dish firmly (you may need help with this as it can be quite heavy) turn the pot upside down on the dish. Leave to stand in a warm place, without moving the pot, for about 15 minutes and then carefully remove the pot. The mixture should retain the mould of the pot, ready for serving. If it collapses, smooth it out on the dish. It still tastes great!

OPTIONS

Serve with natural yoghurt, pitta bread and salad, e.g. the Middle Eastern Salad (see page 144) omitting the feta cheese.

L: Use 4 chicken breast fillets instead of the half chicken/oyster thighs. Chop each fillet into about four or five pieces.

G-F: Some ground spices contain flour to prevent them from sticking together – check the mixed spice label.

HONEYED CHICKEN

This is Chinese inspired and easy to make – chicken marinated in a honey, soy and ginger marinade, then cooked in the oven.

Oven 190°C/375°F/gas mark 5

INGREDIENTS

500g chicken legs/oyster thighs or wings

For the marinade

4-6 cloves of garlic

3cm fresh ginger root

6 tbsp light soy sauce

3 tbsp Chinese rice wine or dry sherry

3 tbsp honey

3 tbsp peanut oil (sunflower or corn oil can be used but peanut oil is best.)

METHOD

1 Crush the garlic and ginger together and mix with the rest of the marinade ingredients in a large non-metal bowl. Add the chicken and mix with the marinade. Refrigerate and leave for two hours, stirring occasionally. If time permits, refrigerate overnight.

2 Place the chicken in an ovenproof dish and cook in the preheated oven for 25-35 minutes until brown and cooked through. Serve immediately with the juices from the oven dish spooned over the chicken.

SHOPPING LIST

chicken, oyster thighs, wings or drumsticks, or chicken breasts if making the leaner version
ginger root
Chinese rice wine or dry sherry
honey

OPTIONS

Serve on their own as a starter, or with boiled rice and stir-fried vegetables as a main course. Sprinkle a little sliced green onion over the chicken.

L: Use chicken breast fillets, sliced in half to make 2 thin fillets, and 1 tbsp oil instead of 3.

C-F: Reduce the garlic by half.

G-F: Check that the soy sauce and sherry are gluten-free.

SAMAKEH HARRAH

Mackerel is so reasonably priced and is such a healthy food that I cook it often. This is a dish from the Levant, which would normally use a lighter fish such as red snapper, but I think mackerel works just as well.

Oven 190°C/375°F/gas mark 5

INGREDIENTS

4 whole, fresh mackerel, scaled, gutted, slit head to tail on one side and spine removed

4 cloves of garlic, crushed

25g fresh coriander, washed and finely chopped

75g walnuts, crushed

juice of 1 lemon

1 tbsp olive oil

¾ tsp salt

1 chilli, chopped very finely

2 tbsp olive oil for brushing over the skin of the fish

SHOPPING LIST

whole, fresh mackerel
fresh coriander
walnuts

METHOD

1 Wash fish and pat dry with kitchen paper. Brush with 2 tbsp olive oil and place on a foil-covered baking tray. Salt the inside lightly.

2 Mix together the garlic, walnuts, chilli, lemon juice, coriander, olive oil and salt and stuff the fish with this.

3 Cover the dish with foil and place in the preheated oven. Bake for 15 minutes. Remove foil and bake for another 10-15 minutes until cooked through. Serve immediately.

OPTIONS

Serve with toasted pitta bread, hommous and Arabic Salad.

L: Serve with a plain salad and without bread.

C-F: The stuffing may be too strong a taste for small children. Cook some of the fish without stuffing and simply salted and brushed with a little oil or butter. Remove all bones and skin before serving. Serve with some salad and toasted pitta.

CURRIED LAMB CHOPS

These lamb chops are delicious heated with the spices and chilli and cooled with creamy yoghurt.

INGREDIENTS

600-800g thin lamb chops

1 large onion, sliced

3-4 cloves of garlic, peeled

2cm fresh ginger root, peeled

1 red or green chilli (optional)

1 small tomato, chopped

2 tbsp sunflower or corn oil

2 tsp hot Madras curry powder

3 small peppers of different colours, at least one of which should be red, seeded and sliced into thin strips

200ml (1 cup) yoghurt

SHOPPING LIST
thin lamb loin chops
root ginger
small peppers of different colours, one of which should be red
yoghurt

METHOD

1 Crush the garlic, ginger root and chilli (if using) together in a pestle and mortar, or chop finely.

2 Heat 1 tbsp of oil in a large pan on medium heat and add the onion. Fry gently for about ten minutes, until the onion softens. Add the garlic/ginger/chilli mixture. Stir fry for a couple of minutes. Add the curry powder and cook for a minute, stirring.

3 Remove all from the pan and set aside. Scrape any food residue to the side with a spatula.

4 Add the other tbsp oil to the pan and increase the heat to high. Sear the chops on each side for one minute. Reduce the heat to medium and fry for another 1½-2 minutes each side, depending on the thickness of the chops.

5 Add the peppers and stir fry for a minute or two. Add the tomato and then add back the fried onion mixture and stir all together.

6 Push the lamb chops to the side of the pan and add the yoghurt. Stir until it heats up – a minute or two – and then mix everything together.

7 Reduce the heat, cover and cook for about 5 minutes, stirring once or twice.

OPTIONS

Serve with boiled rice.

L: Trim the lamb of all fat and use low-fat yoghurt.

C-F: This curry could be too strong a taste for small children. Cook their lamb chops without sauce and serve chopped up in small pieces with a little plain yoghurt and rice.

G-F: Some curry powders and yoghurts contain gluten – check the label.

Note: *Any thinly sliced lamb that is tender enough to fry is suitable here, e.g. cutlets, loin chops, leg chops or neck fillets.*

SWEET & SOUR PRAWNS

Prawns are very often on special offer – and where possible details will be on the shrewdfood.ie website. These prawns can be cooked with or without batter, depending on individual taste. Cooking with batter takes longer, so here I'm taking the easy road and cooking them without it. I'm also using cooked prawns for an easier life.

INGREDIENTS

500g small cooked prawns

3-4 cloves of garlic, chopped

2cm fresh ginger root, peeled

4 scallions, chopped diagonally

I red and I green pepper, cut into I cm slices

I ½ tbsp peanut, sunflower or corn oil

For the sauce

2 tbsp Chinese rice wine or dry sherry

2 tbsp sugar

2 tbsp vinegar

3 tbsp soy sauce

I ½ tbsp tomato paste

½ tbsp cornflour, mixed until smooth with a little water

SHOPPING LIST

prawns
ginger root
scallions
red and green peppers
Chinese rice wine or dry sherry

METHOD

1 Mix all the sauce ingredients together.

2 Heat the oil in a large seasoned frying pan or wok. When it starts to smoke, add the garlic and ginger, stirring together for about half a minute.

3 Add the scallions and peppers and stir fry for a minute before adding the prawns. Mix all together and cook for another minute or so.

4 Pour in the sauce and stir. Cook for a couple of minutes, stirring until the sauce thickens.

5 Cover and turn off the heat. Leave on the hot stove for about 3 minutes, until the prawns are thoroughly heated through.

OPTIONS

Serve with boiled rice and prawn crackers.

C-F: Remove some of the prawns from the sauce and serve with rice and prawn crackers.

G-F: Check that the soy sauce, dry sherry and cornflour are gluten-free. Use plain distilled vinegar – not malt, which can contain gluten.

KEDGEREE

I believe this is an Indian dish originally, although there are those who say that it is a Scottish dish which was taken to India during the days of the British Raj. In Victorian England, it was used as a breakfast dish, but this is my dinner version.

INGREDIENTS

500g smoked haddock or coley

4 hard-boiled eggs

425ml (2½ cups) of long-grained or basmati rice, washed and drained (if starchy, soak for 30 minutes)

2 medium onions, chopped

1 tbsp freshly chopped parsley

1 carrot, chopped

1 stick of celery, chopped

500mls (2½ cups) of water

4 tbsp butter

1 large tomato, chopped

2 tsp hot Madras curry powder

¼ tsp cayenne pepper

salt and freshly ground black pepper

a little fresh, chopped coriander to serve

METHOD

1 Hard-boil the eggs. When cooled, shell, quarter and set aside.

2 Place chopped parsley, carrot, celery and one of the onions into a saucepan with the water. Bring to the boil. Cover and simmer for about 15 minutes until the vegetables are cooked. Add the fish and simmer for about 5 minutes until cooked through. Remove the fish and strain the stock, discarding the vegetables. If necessary add water to bring the stock back to 500mls (2½ cups) of liquid.

3 Remove the skin and any bones from the fish, and break up into pieces about 2cm square. Set aside and keep warm.

4 Heat the butter in a saucepan until it begins to foam, then quickly add the remaining onion. Fry gently until softened and add the spices. Fry for about a minute together, stirring, and then add the tomato and a little salt. Fry gently for another minute, then add the rice and the fish stock. Bring to the boil and stir. Cover and reduce the heat to the lowest setting. Cook until the rice is soft – about 15 minutes. Stir again when cooked to separate the grains.

5 Add the fish and mix together gently. Check the seasoning and serve immediately on a large, heated platter, decorated with the quartered eggs and with the coriander scattered on top.

> **Note:** *See page 227 for tips on making perfect hard-boiled eggs.*

OPTIONS

Serve with plain yoghurt or tsatsiki and naan bread.

L: Replace the butter with 3 tbsp oil, and serve with low-fat yoghurt and without the bread.

C-F: The taste of smoked fish may be too strong for some children, in which case they can be served some rice with yoghurt and half a boiled egg, chopped. A little bit of fish can be added to try.

G-F: Check that the curry powder and cayenne are gluten-free.

SHOPPING LIST

smoked haddock or coley
fresh parsley
carrot
celery
fresh coriander

PORK & VEGETABLE STIR FRY

I simply love a stir fry and this is one of my favourites. Deliciously tender pork with lots of crunchy vegetables and a lovely, garlicky, meaty sauce. If you don't have time to marinate the meat overnight, simply leave it to infuse while you chop the vegetables. Here I used only half a pork steak, and put the rest in the freezer to have another day, with different vegetables.

INGREDIENTS

Meat and marinade

300-400g pork steak, trimmed of any fat and cut into pieces about 1cm wide and about 3cm long

5-6 large cloves of garlic, chopped

1½ tbsp of white vinegar

1½ tbsp light soy sauce

1 tsp sugar

½ tsp Szechuan pepper (if unavailable use ordinary white pepper)

½ tbsp toasted sesame oil

½ tbsp peanut oil

Sauce

1 tsp cornflour

150ml (¾ cup) chicken or vegetable stock

a knob of butter

Other ingredients

1 medium onion, sliced

3 medium carrots, sliced

150g mushrooms, sliced

125g broccoli, sliced

3 tbsp sunflower oil

METHOD

1 Mix the steak with the marinade ingredients and refrigerate for at least 30 minutes, but preferably overnight or even for 24 hours.

2 Heat 1 tbsp oil in a wok (or large frying pan) and add mushrooms. Stir fry for 3-4 minutes until a little crisp. Salt and set aside.

3 Add 1 tbsp oil to the wok and heat until smoking. Add carrots and onions and stir fry for 1½ minutes. Add the broccoli and stir fry for one minute more. Remove from pan and set aside.

4 Heat last tbsp oil in the wok until smoking, add the meat and stir fry on high for two minutes. Add the mushrooms and vegetables, stir and cook for another two minutes on high. Mix the sauce ingredients, add to the pan and stir until the sauce thickens. Cover, cook for another minute and remove from the heat.

OPTIONS

Serve with boiled rice or noodles.

L: Omit the butter.

G-F: Check that the Szechuan pepper, soy sauce, vinegar, sesame oil, cornflour and stock are gluten-free.

SHOPPING LIST
pork steak
toasted sesame oil
carrots
mushrooms
broccoli

PORK CHOPS & PEPPERS

Pork chops are often on special offer and this recipe is easy to prepare. You can get away with marinating the pork chops for about half an hour, but if you can do them overnight it's worth it – they will be amazingly juicy and tender.

INGREDIENTS

Meat and marinade

4 pork chops about 2cm thick

70mls (⅓ cup) sweet chilli sauce

1½ tbsp cider vinegar

2 tbsp sunflower or corn oil

a good dash of black pepper

Other ingredients

3 peppers, small, differently coloured peppers, sliced 1cm thick

50mls (¼ cup) sweet chilli sauce

1 tbsp sunflower or corn oil for stir frying

1 large white onion, peeled, sliced 1cm thick and slices separated.

METHOD

1 Mix the chops with the marinade ingredients and refrigerate for at least 30 minutes, but preferably overnight or even for 24 hours.

2 Heat 1 tbsp oil in a wok or heavy pan until it begins to smoke a little. Add the onions and stir fry for about two minutes. Add the peppers and stir fry for half a minute. Stir in the sweet chilli sauce and transfer to a warmed plate. Cover and keep hot in a slightly heated oven while you cook the chops.

3 Add the remaining tbsp oil to the pan and heat until it begins to smoke. Add the chops, but not the marinade, and sear each side for a minute. Turn the heat down to medium and cook for a further **3** minutes approx. each side, turning to keep from burning, until cooked through. Transfer to a warmed plate in the oven. Add any leftover marinade juice to the pan and bring to the boil. Pour this sauce over the chops.

OPTIONS

Serve the chops, with the peppers, over mashed potatoes, drizzling the sauce over both. Add other vegetables such as peas, broccoli or Brussels sprouts if desired. Also good with boiled rice

L: Trim the pork chops of any fat and reduce the oil to 1 tbsp in total.

G-F: Use gluten-free sweet chilli sauce and gluten-free cider vinegar.

SHOPPING LIST
pork chops
sweet chilli sauce
peppers, of different colours

HONEY PORK CHOPS

A little advance preparation can transform this dish, as the chops will become more tender and tasty if they are left in the marinade overnight.

INGREDIENTS

4 pork chops, preferably on the bone

4 tbsp light soy sauce

2 tsp mustard powder

4 tbsp honey

2 tbsp vinegar

2 cloves of garlic, chopped

2 tbsp sunflower or corn oil for frying

a mixture of sliced vegetables for stir frying, e.g. onions, peppers, mangetout, baby corn

SHOPPING LIST

pork chops

a mixture of vegetables to stir fry, e.g. onions, peppers, mangetout, baby corn, broccoli, carrots

honey

METHOD

1 In a bowl, mix the pork chops with all the ingredients except the oil and vegetables.

2 Cover and refrigerate for at least 2 hours and preferably overnight.

3 Remove from the marinade and pat dry with kitchen paper.

4 Heat 1 tbsp oil in a large frying pan until just beginning to smoke and immediately add the pork chops. Fry for one minute on each side and then reduce the heat to medium and cook for a further 3 minutes approx. each side, turning to keep from burning, until cooked through. Remove from the pan and keep warm.

5 Turn up the heat to maximum and add 1 tbsp oil to the pan. Stir fry the vegetables for about a minute. Pour the marinade over the vegetables (they should be hot enough to sizzle) and cook for a minute or so. Serve immediately, with the pork chops.

OPTIONS

Serve with mashed potato or boiled rice.

L: Trim the pork chops of any fat, and use low-fat soy sauce.

G-F: Ensure that the soy sauce, mustard and vinegar are gluten-free.

SHREWD
AMERICAS

This section is predominantly American, North and South. The combination of travel, television and the internet has given us the opportunity to further explore the cuisines of other countries.

The recipes in this section conform to the Shrewd Food ethos of being inexpensive, easy to make and very tasty, and of course they are, like all the recipes in this book, based on special offers that are repeated regularly in our supermarkets. Some of them may be new to you, as they use our everyday ingredients in different and unusual combinations to provide a smorgasbord of tastes and textures – enjoy!

DEEP SOUTH HAM & SWEET POTATOES

This is my version of the classic deep south dish. Honey glazed, mildly spiced ham and sweet potato with the faintest tang of orange. This can be prepared ahead and stored in an oven dish in the fridge, ready to pop in the oven about 45 minutes before dinner. Ham fillets offer good value generally, and are often on special offer.

Oven 190°C/375°F/gas mark 5

INGREDIENTS

1.5-1.8kg ham fillet

½ a vegetable stock cube

½ tbsp honey plus 65ml (⅓ cup) for the sauce

¼ tsp mixed spice for cooking the ham and ¼ tsp for the sauce

500g sweet potato (approx. 1 large potato)

65ml (⅓ cup) orange juice

25g butter

black pepper

METHOD

Soak ham overnight in cold water. Rinse and add the ½ stock cube, ½ tbsp honey and ¼ tsp of mixed spice. Cover with cold water and bring to the boil. Reduce heat and simmer for 30 minutes per ½ kilo. Remove from the heat and set aside.

2 Bring about 4cm salted water to the boil in a saucepan. Peel and slice the sweet potato into 1cm slices. Add to the boiling water, return to the boil and reduce the heat. Simmer for 5 to 10 minutes, until cooked but still firm. Drain and leave aside.

3 Remove the ham from the stock and slice about 1cm thick. Cut each slice in half.

4 Heat the butter in an oven dish and add the rest of the honey, orange juice and the remaining $\frac{1}{4}$ tsp mixed spice.

5 Layer the ham and the sweet potato in the dish and baste with the honey mixture. Grate a little black pepper over the top. Put into the oven and bake (basting every 10 minutes) for 35-40 minutes.

OPTIONS

Serve with sautéed greens of your choice and/or boiled rice, spooning a little of the sauce from the dish over each serving of rice. It's also great with chips or plain wedges.

L: Use half the amount of butter.

G-F: Ensure that the ham, stock and spice are gluten-free.

SHOPPING LIST

ham fillet
honey
sweet potato
orange juice

BEEFBURGERS

Hamburgers or beefburgers, possibly American's most famous food, used to be made with cheap ground beef, but in more recent affluent times they tended to be made from steak mince. I think they can taste every bit as good with an ordinary mince, and it's better value.

INGREDIENTS

500g fairly lean beef mince

1 tsp mustard powder

½ tsp freshly ground black pepper

¾ tsp salt

2 medium onions, chopped

1 tbsp any oil except olive oil

2 thick slices of good bread, crumbed (I use a crusty cob)

1 tbsp milk

2 tbsp oil for frying

SHOPPING LIST

lean beef mince

bread, batch or cob

METHOD

1 Heat the oil in a pan. Add the onions and cook until golden brown. Leave to cool.

2 Put all the other ingredients into a bowl and add the cooled, cooked onions. Mix together thoroughly and form into burgers about 1½cm thick.

3 Heat the rest of the oil and cook the burgers for about 5 minutes each side, turning frequently, until cooked through.

OPTIONS

Serve with burger buns, salad, mayonnaise, ketchup, chips.

L: Instead of frying the burgers, brush them lightly with oil and grill on high until cooked through. Serve with a plain salad and without buns or chips.

G-F: Use gluten-free bread or half a gluten-free bagel for the breadcrumbs and burger buns. Ensure the mustard powder is gluten-free.

C-F: Use half the amount of mustard and pepper.

MEATBALLS

Meatballs go back centuries. The ancient Romans made them. So did the Turks and the Persians and they are still a very popular modern dish. The two important things to get right are tenderness and moistness. Using a good quality mince solves the first problem, and I find that baking them, instead of frying them, helps stop them drying out.

Oven 165°C/325°F/gas mark 3

INGREDIENTS

500g good quality lean beef mince

1-2 large cloves of garlic, peeled and crushed

3 tbsp chopped fresh parsley

½ tsp dried thyme

½ tsp dried basil

1 small slice of good quality bread, crumbed

20g (¼ cup) grated Parmesan

⅓ of a beef stock cube dissolved in 50ml (¼ cup) water

1 tbsp vinegar

a little oil for cooking

SHOPPING LIST

good quality lean beef mince
fresh parsley
bread

METHOD

1 Mix the ingredients together. Form into balls a little smaller than a ping pong ball.

2 Put on a lightly oiled oven dish and place in a preheated oven. Turn after 10 minutes. Bake for another 15 minutes until cooked through.

OPTIONS

Serve with tomato sauce (see page 150) and pasta or rice.

L: Use extra-lean mince and serve with salad instead of pasta or rice.

G-F: Use gluten-free bread or one quarter of a gluten-free bagel for the breadcrumbs. Make sure the stock, Parmesan and vinegar are gluten-free. Serve with gluten-free pasta.

C-F: Some children find Parmesan too strong tasting, in which case just leave it out.

CHILLI CON CARNE

Chilli con carne combines many flavours into one hearty dish. It is a universal favourite and great to come home to on a cold night. Don't be put off by the somewhat long list of ingredients – most of them are just thrown in together.

INGREDIENTS

500g beef mince

1 large onion, chopped

1 green pepper, deseeded and chopped into 1cm squares

3 cloves of garlic, peeled and chopped

½ tsp dried oregano

1 tsp ground coriander

1½ tsp paprika

¾ tsp ground cumin

½-1 tsp chilli powder, depending on how hot you want it

1 tsp cocoa powder

½ tsp sugar

1 tsp Worcestershire sauce

1 tin chopped tomatoes

1 tin kidney beans

70mls (⅓ cup) vegetable or chicken stock

1 tsp Tabasco sauce

1 tbsp oil

salt and freshly ground black pepper

SHOPPING LIST

beef mince
green pepper
cocoa powder
tinned chopped tomatoes
kidney beans

METHOD

1 Heat the oil in a saucepan and lightly fry the onion, without browning.

2 Add the garlic and green pepper and stir fry for a couple of minutes. Using a slotted spoon, remove the onion, garlic and pepper to a warm plate and add the mince, spices and herbs. Stir to prevent it sticking together, and cook until the mince has browned. Return the onion, garlic and pepper to the saucepan and stir together.

3 Add the cocoa, sugar, Worcestershire sauce, tomatoes, kidney beans and stock and bring to a simmer. Reduce the heat immediately, cover and simmer gently for about 45 minutes, stirring occasionally.

4 Stir in the Tabasco and heat through for about 5 minutes.

OPTIONS

Serve with boiled rice or crusty bread.

L: Use extra lean mince, or chicken or turkey breast mince.

C-F: Make with half the amount of chilli powder and Tabasco or leave them out altogether.

G-F: Ensure the stock, spices and cocoa used are gluten-free. Use distilled vinegar instead of Worcestershire sauce.

Note: *It is important not to boil the tomatoes, as they will become bitter.*

SMOKED COLEY CHOWDER

This soup is great on its own or you can add some diced carrots with the potatoes, or throw in a small can of sweetcorn, drained, with the coley.

INGREDIENTS

750g smoked coley

50g butter

1 large white onion, chopped

1 leek, cut into 1cm slices

6 medium potatoes in 1cm cubes

750ml (3½ cups) chicken stock

750ml milk

1½ tbsp chopped fresh parsley

SHOPPING LIST

smoked coley

leek

potatoes

fresh parsley

Note: *This is a great dish to make if you have people arriving home at different times. Just make the recipe as far as step 2 and take out individual servings, adding fish and parsley as each person arrives home so it is deliciously fresh each time. Add a dollop of fresh cream as a treat.*

METHOD

1 Melt the butter in a large saucepan and add the onions and leeks. Cook gently without browning until soft, about 10 minutes.

2 Add potatoes, stock and milk. Bring back to the boil and simmer until the potatoes are barely cooked.

3 Check the coley for bones and remove any. Add to the stock and bring to the boil. Simmer for about 3 minutes, add parsley and remove from heat. Serve immediately.

OPTIONS

Serve with crusty rolls or bread of your choice.

L: Replace the butter with 1 tbsp olive oil. Use low-fat milk and reduce the number of potatoes to 3.

C-F: Children may not like the taste of smoked fish – add a little extra milk to help dilute it. Make sure all fish bones have been removed before serving to children.

G-F: Use a gluten-free stock.

CRANBERRY CHICKEN

The bite of cranberry and the sweetness of the sugar gives this chicken great zing. You can use skinless chicken breasts if you like, but I prefer the juicier thighs.

Oven 200°C/400°F/gas mark 6

INGREDIENTS

1-1.5kg oyster thighs, trimmed of excess skin and fat, skinned if preferred. Chicken legs or drumsticks can be used instead

1 medium onion, finely chopped

15g butter

½ tbsp oil

100ml (½ cup) tomato ketchup

75g (⅓ cup) brown sugar

⅔ tsp mustard powder

15ml cider vinegar

150ml (¾ cup) cranberry sauce – whole cranberry if possible

SHOPPING LIST

chicken oyster thighs, legs or drumsticks
cranberry sauce (whole if available)

METHOD

1 Heat oil and half the butter in a saucepan or, if you have one, a flameproof oven dish. Add the onion and cook gently until transparent.

2 Place the onion in an oven dish and cover with the chicken, skin side up. Rub the chicken with the rest of the butter. Bake for 30 minutes.

3 Meanwhile mix all the other ingredients together.

4 Remove the chicken from the oven and spoon the cranberry mixture over it. Return it to the oven for around 20 minutes, basting after 10, until the sauce is a little caramelised, and the chicken is cooked through.

5 Spoon off any excess oil and serve with the juices.

OPTIONS

Serve with boiled rice and stir-fried vegetables, or with mashed potatoes and green beans or broccoli.

L: Use chicken breasts instead of oyster thighs and ½ tbsp oil instead of the butter.

G-F: Ensure the ketchup, vinegar and cranberry sauce are gluten-free.

HONEY ROAST HAM

I usually cook a big ham so that I can have some left over for sandwiches and salads. This recipe would feed 6-8 for dinner. If you don't use it all on the day, you could freeze the leftovers if you don't have any immediate need for them. I slice the leftover ham and divide it up into small bags for the freezer, where it will keep for up to two months.

Oven 190°C/375°F/gas mark 5

INGREDIENTS

2kg ham

1 vegetable stock cube

3 tbsp honey

1 tsp mustard powder

salt and freshly ground black pepper

3-4 tbsp stock in which the ham was cooked

SHOPPING LIST

ham

honey

METHOD

1 Soak the ham overnight in water.

2 Discard water, put the ham in a saucepan and cover with cold water. Add the vegetable stock cube and bring to the boil slowly. Cook for 1 hour and 35 minutes and leave to cool in the stock for 30 minutes.

3 Meanwhile prepare the glaze by mixing the honey, mustard and a shake of black pepper together. Remove the ham from the stock carefully, as it is rolled and could come apart. Remove most of the fat and smear with the glaze. Put on an oven tray and add 3-4 tbsp the cooking stock. Place in the preheated oven for 25-30 minutes, basting with the stock and juices every 10 minutes.

4 Allow to rest for 10 minutes before carving.

OPTIONS

Serve hot with green vegetables and baked potatoes. When cold it can be served with salad and baked potatoes or potato salad. Leftovers can be refrigerated and used for sandwiches and salads.

G-F: Use gluten-free ham and stock.

SMOKED HAM & PEAS

This one is so easy that you could do it while writing a best-selling novel, putting up a bookshelf and helping the kids with their homework. And it's delicious!

INGREDIENTS

1kg smoked ham fillet

260g (1½ cups) blackeye peas

1 vegetable stock cube

juice of quarter of a lemon

½ tbsp flat leaf parsley, chopped

SHOPPING LIST

smoked ham fillet
dried blackeye peas
flat leaf parsley

METHOD

1 Soak ham and peas, separately, overnight in cold water. Drain and rinse the ham. Put into a pot, just about cover with cold water and add the stock cube. Bring to the boil and simmer until cooked, approx. 1½ hours.

2 Strain most of the stock into another pot and boil until the liquid reduces by half.

3 Drain the beans, add to the ham stock and cook until soft, which could take from 15 to thirty minutes.

4 Cut the ham into slices or pieces and add to the beans. Simmer together for about 10 minutes, add the lemon juice and the chopped parsley and serve.

OPTIONS

Serve with baked or mashed potatoes, or a bread of your choice to soak up the tangy juices.

L: Trim any fat from the ham.

G-F: Use gluten-free ham and stock.

LEEK & SAUSAGE CHICKEN

Spicy sausage and leek stuffing enfolded in thin chicken breast, pan-fried for colour and finished off in the oven. Scrumptious!

Oven 180°C/350°F/gas mark 4

INGREDIENTS

4 chicken breast fillets

1 leek

3-4 sausages

25g (½ cup) of breadcrumbs

1 tbsp margarine

½ tbsp freshly chopped parsley

a few fresh thyme leaves or ¼ tsp dried thyme

salt and white pepper

4 cocktail sticks

SHOPPING LIST

chicken breast fillets
leek
sausages
breadcrumbs
margarine
fresh parsley
fresh thyme (if using)

METHOD

1 Trim the leek, wash it and cut into ½cm rings. Heat about 2cm salted water in a small saucepan and add the leeks. Simmer until tender, drain and set aside to cool a little.

2 Heat about a third of the margarine in a frying pan and cook the sausages until brown all over.

3 Transfer sausages to a plate and cut into ½cm rings. Don't wash the pan – keep if for the chicken.

4 Mix the breadcrumbs, parsley and thyme together and rub in the remainder of the margarine. Add the cooled leeks and chopped sausages and mix all together. Season a little, but be careful not to overdo it as the sausages will add quite a bit of seasoning.

5 Place a tray in the oven to heat.

6 Slit each chicken fillet in half lengthways, but don't cut all the way through. Open out the fillets like a book and pound until less than 1cm thick. Season lightly with salt and pepper and divide the filling among the fillets. Fold the chicken around the stuffing and secure with a cocktail stick.

7 Reheat the frying pan and sear the stuffed fillets for 2 minutes on each side. Transfer to the heated oven tray, and cook in the preheated oven for about 12 minutes. Cover with foil and remove to a warm place – the opened oven door is good – for 5 minutes. Slice the chicken and serve immediately.

OPTIONS

Serve with sautéed greens of your choice and/or boiled rice, spooning a little of the sauce from the dish over each serving of rice. It's also great with chips or plain wedges.

L: Use half the amount of butter.

G-F: Ensure that the sausages are gluten-free. Use gluten-free breadcrumbs.

CELERY CHEESE CHICKEN

Oven 165°C/325°F/gas mark 3

Oven dish 30cm x 20cm x 5cm deep, approx.

INGREDIENTS

4 chicken breasts

4 sticks of celery, sliced lengthways and finely chopped

1 large onion, finely chopped

1 tbsp flour or cornflour

30g butter

250ml (1 ¼ cups) milk

50g extra mature or vintage Cheddar, grated

SHOPPING LIST

chicken breasts

celery

extra mature or vintage Cheddar

METHOD

1 Use a little of the butter to grease your oven dish.

2 Trim the chicken breasts of any fat or gristle. Slice each chicken breast in two lengthways, so that you have 8 thin pieces of chicken. Cut each piece in half and place the pieces in the oven dish.

3 Heat the rest of the butter in a saucepan until it begins to foam. Add the onions and celery, and cook gently until they soften – about 10 minutes.

4 Meanwhile mix the flour or cornflour with a little of the milk. When blended, mix in the rest of the milk. Add to the onions and celery and stir until the sauce thickens. Add the cheese and stir until it melts into the sauce. Season liberally with salt and pepper to taste, bearing in mind that it will be a little diluted when you add it to the chicken. Set aside and allow to cool slightly.

5 When the sauce has cooled a little, spoon over the chicken and place in the preheated oven. Bake for 35-40 minutes, until the chicken is cooked through and is no longer pink inside, and the top is beginning to turn slightly golden. Serve while hot.

OPTIONS

Serve with boiled rice, or tortilla wraps and chopped peppers.

L: Replace the butter with 2 tbsp olive oil, use low-fat milk and low-fat cheese.

G-F: Use gluten-free cornflour for the sauce.

SOUTH AMERICAN PORK WITH LIME

We're off to South America here. This is a lovely, spicy tangy way to cook pork steak. Tenderloin pork is frequently on offer. If time permits, marinate the pork steak overnight in the spices and the end result will be even better.

Oven 210°C/410°F/gas mark 6½

INGREDIENTS

2 small pork tenderloins, 500-600g each

4 good-sized garlic cloves, peeled

2 tsp paprika

1 tsp ground cumin

1 tsp dried mixed herbs

1 tbsp oil and a little extra to rub on the oven tray

1 lime

2 tbsp mayonnaise

salt and freshly ground black pepper

lettuce and salad to serve

SHOPPING LIST

pork tenderloin

lime

lettuce and salad of choice

OPTIONS

Good with rice, salad and French fries, and indeed most vegetables.

L: Use low-fat mayonnaise.

C-F: Rub a portion of the tenderloin with a very small amount of garlic and spice. Shred the lettuce and cut the salad ingredients into small pieces. Use a small amount of mayonnaise.

METHOD

1 Trim the tenderloins of any fat.

2 Crush the garlic in a pestle and mortar. Mix in the paprika, cumin, mixed herbs, oil and a little salt and black pepper. Rub the meat with this paste, cover and leave in the fridge for at least 30 minutes and preferably overnight.

3 Rub an oven tray with a little oil and place the tenderloins on it. Roast in the preheated oven for about 30 minutes until the steaks are cooked though.

4 While the pork is cooking, grate the skin of the lime and keep aside. Squeeze the juice of half of the lime and mix it, with the zest, into the mayonnaise. Keep mixing until the mayonnaise is smooth.

5 Remove the pork from the oven and allow to rest for 5 minutes.

6 Arrange some washed lettuce and salad on 4 plates. Slice the pork tenderloins 1½cm thick and place them on the lettuce. Spoon the mayonnaise over the pork and salad and serve.

SHREWD
VEGETARIAN

Although I am not a vegetarian, I have been a lover of vegetables and salads since childhood. Growing up, we had the best of fresh, home-grown vegetables as my mother was a keen gardener and my father grew the spuds and the swedes.

In summer we had delicious salads with home-grown scallions and lettuce, picked just half an hour before tea, and home-made soda bread and butter.

Vegetables are the ultimate shrewd food. They are not only a healthy option, they are also economical – especially when bought in season – and are significantly cheaper than meat. From both a health and a budget perspective, I often add an extra vegetarian dish to meals. And of course if we are to ensure that no one in the world goes hungry, we should all be eating more vegetables and less meat.

CAULIFLOWER CHEESE

This is comfort food at its best. A very mature or vintage Cheddar is essential. This is my basic recipe. Sometimes I add a few chopped chives or scallions, or a little chopped, fresh parsley.

Oven 200°C/400°F/gas mark 6

INGREDIENTS

1 large cauliflower, washed and cut into florets

50g butter

1 tbsp flour or cornflour

½ tsp English mustard powder

150-175g mature Cheddar cheese

300ml milk

a pinch cayenne pepper

25g grated Parmesan cheese

salt and white pepper

SHOPPING LIST

cauliflower

mature Cheddar cheese

METHOD

1 Blanch the cauliflower florets in boiling salted water, and simmer for about 5 minutes. Drain and place in a buttered oven dish.

2 Heat the butter in a saucepan until it begins to foam. Add the flour or cornflour and stir until it forms a paste. Cook gently for 2 minutes, stirring all the time. Whisk in the milk gradually, stirring all the time, until the mixture thickens to a smooth sauce.

3 Reduce the heat and add the Cheddar, cayenne, mustard and salt and white pepper, and stir until the cheese melts.

4 Spoon the sauce over the cauliflower, top with the grated Parmesan and bake for 15-20 minutes until golden brown and bubbling.

OPTIONS

Serve with wholemeal bread and green vegetables.

L: Replace butter with 2 tbsp olive oil and cheese with a low-fat version. Use low-fat milk.

G-F: Use gluten-free cornflour, mustard and cayenne. Check the Parmesan and if a gluten-free product is not available, use the same amount of grated, extra mature Cheddar.

TIAN D'AUBERGINES

This is a very simple tian, but nothing has been lost in terms of taste. The aubergines and cheese bubble up through the tomatoes and onions on the top and the result is sublime.

Oven 165°C/325°F/gas mark 3

Oven dish 25cm x 15cm x 5cm deep, approx.

INGREDIENTS

2 medium to large aubergines

sunflower or corn oil to fry the aubergines

250g mozzarella, chopped

75g medium Cheddar, grated

2 eggs

4 ripe, medium-sized tomatoes, washed and quartered

1 medium onion, peeled and quartered

salt and black pepper

SHOPPING LIST

aubergines
mozzarella
medium Cheddar

METHOD

1 Peel and slice the aubergines, about 1cm thick. Add cold water and 1 tbsp salt to a bowl big enough to hold the aubergines. Put the aubergines into the salted water, covering with a plate to keep them submerged, and soak for 30 minutes. Drain and pat dry with kitchen paper.

2 Heat enough oil in a saucepan or pan to deep fry the aubergines. Deep fry them in batches until they are golden in colour. Drain on kitchen paper and set aside.

3 Chop the onion and tomatoes finely (or whiz them in a blender). Beat the eggs quickly and add to the onion and tomato. Season the mixture with salt and pepper.

4 Layer your oven dish with the aubergines and cheeses and season well. Pour the tomato/onion/egg mixture over the aubergine and cheese.

5 Bake in a preheated oven for one hour.

OPTIONS

Serve with crusty rolls or wholemeal bread. Great with potatoes too and can also be served as a side dish.

L: Use a low-fat mozzarella and Cheddar.

G-F: Check that the mozzarella is gluten-free.

RATATOUILLE

I would advise cooking a great big pot of this as it can be eaten hot or cold and will keep in the fridge for several days. It's originally a Niçoise dish, and the combination of fresh vegetables and olive oil is not only delicious, but also amazingly healthy. Don't get too hung up on how big or small the ingredients should be chopped – just chuck 'em in – but it is crucial to cook everything slowly, and not to let the vegetables boil as this makes them bitter. It also needs generous seasoning, which should be done as the ingredients are added.

INGREDIENTS

2 medium to large onions, chopped

6 cloves of garlic, chopped

2-3 tbsp olive oil

2 peppers, ideally 1 red, 1 green, washed, deseeded and roughly chopped

5-6 medium to large tomatoes (ideally vine tomatoes), washed and chopped roughly

2 medium courgettes, washed and sliced into 2cm lengths

2 medium aubergines, washed and cut into chunks approx. 2cm square

1-2 tsp dried herbes de Provence (or dried mixed herbs)

salt and freshly ground black pepper

METHOD

1 Heat olive oil in a large saucepan and sauté the onions and garlic for half a minute. Turn the heat down, add a little salt, and cook gently for about 10 minutes until the onions are soft.

2 Turn up the heat a little and add the peppers and stir. Simmer gently for 5 minutes.

3 Add the tomatoes and a little salt and bring almost to a boil, turning the heat down immediately to a gentle simmer. Cook for 15 minutes.

4 Add the courgettes and simmer for 5-10 minutes.

5 Add the aubergines, the herbs, salt if necessary and some black pepper and stir. Cover and simmer very gently for another hour.

6 Adjust seasoning and serve.

OPTIONS

Serve with crusty bread and butter, or over rice. Serve cold as a salad.

SHOPPING LIST

peppers, ideally red and green
tomatoes (preferably vine)
courgettes
aubergines
dried herbes de Provence (if using)

MIDDLE EASTERN SALAD

This salad is popular in many Mediterranean countries. The mixture of fresh salad ingredients with olive oil, lemon and garlic is not only refreshingly tasty, but is full of goodness too. The Lebanese, famous for their 'chudr' or greens, serve this type of salad with almost every meal. The addition of feta is Greek and this makes it into a meal on its own.

INGREDIENTS

1 200g packet of feta cheese, drained and broken into chunks

1 small cos lettuce, leaves separated and washed

½ cucumber, washed

2-3 medium vine tomatoes, washed

½ bunch scallions, trimmed and washed

1 large clove of garlic, peeled and crushed

juice of 1 lemon

65ml (⅓ cup) of good quality olive oil

50g fresh flat leafed parsley, washed and finely chopped

a few mint leaves, washed and finely chopped

salt

SHOPPING LIST

feta cheese
cos lettuce
cucumber
tomatoes (preferably vine)
scallions
flat leaf parsley
fresh mint

METHOD

1 Chop the cucumber, the scallions and the tomatoes into small pieces about the size of a pea and mix together in a bowl with the parsley and mint.

2 Mix the garlic, lemon juice and olive oil together and season well with salt.

3 Cut the cos into strips about 3cm wide and place in a large bowl. Break the feta into pieces about 3cm square and sprinkle through the lettuce.

4 Just before serving, mix the lemon, garlic and oil dressing with the tomatoes, cucumber etc. and pour over the lettuce and feta.

OPTIONS

Serve with toasted pitta bread or any crusty bread or rolls.

C-F: I always find that children like salad better if it's chopped small and served with bread, rice or potato.

G-F: Some feta cheeses contain rennet, which may contain gluten – always check the label.

COURGETTE PASTA

This is an incredibly uncomplicated and easy-to-make pasta recipe. Don't be fooled by the small amount of ingredients. Just simple, just delicious!

INGREDIENTS

400g pasta of your choice

4 courgettes, grated

4 large cloves of garlic, chopped

4 medium tomatoes, chopped

2½ tbsp corn or sunflower oil

salt and freshly ground black pepper

a little grated Parmesan or chopped mozzarella (optional)

a little chopped parsley, to serve

SHOPPING LIST

courgettes
mozzarella, if using
fresh parsley

METHOD

1 Cook the pasta al dente in a large saucepan of boiling salted water (add ½ tbsp oil to the water to avoid it sticking together).

2 In a separate saucepan, heat the remaining 2 tbsp of oil. Add the garlic and courgettes and sauté over a high heat for a minute. Reduce the heat to medium, add a little salt, and stir.

3 Cook gently, without browning, for 5 minutes more. Add the tomatoes and stir. Cook gently for another 5 minutes, stirring occasionally. Check the seasoning, adding salt and pepper if necessary.

4 Toss with the pasta, sprinkle with cheese and parsley and serve immediately.

OPTIONS

Serve with buttered, crusty rolls, or toast.

L: Reduce the oil to 1 tbsp to cook the courgettes, and omit the oil in the pasta. Serve with low-fat cheese.

G-F: Use a gluten-free pasta and if gluten-free Parmesan or mozzarella are not available, use the same quantity of grated, extra mature Cheddar.

ASPARAGUS & SCALLION SALAD

This tasty salad can be served warm, or refrigerated and served chilled. It is full-flavoured yet very light.

INGREDIENTS

3-4 bunches of fresh asparagus, 600-800g

3 bunches scallions

3 tbsp red wine vinegar

3 tbsp good olive oil

4 hard-boiled eggs

salt and freshly ground black pepper

SHOPPING LIST

asparagus

scallions

METHOD

1 Wash the asparagus and snap off the ends about 10cm from the bottom, they will snap off naturally at the correct point.

2 Cut the roots off the scallions, trim any wilted parts and wash.

3 Put the asparagus into a large pot of boiling water, making sure there is enough water to cover them. Bring to the boil and simmer for 3-4 minutes until the asparagus is cooked but firm. Remove with a slotted spoon, place in a colander and rinse with cold water. Set aside.

4 Bring the water in the saucepan back to the boil and add the scallions. Blanch for one minute in the boiling water. Drain and rinse with cold water. Cut the cooked asparagus and the scallions into pieces about 1cm long and put into a bowl.

5 Meanwhile, make the dressing. Put the remaining ingredients, except the eggs, into a jar, close and shake until mixed. An old jam jar, which has been washed, is perfect for this.

6 Remove the shells from the hard-boiled eggs and chop. Add to the asparagus and scallions and mix in the dressing. Season with salt and black pepper and serve.

OPTIONS

This is perfect served with crusty rolls or wholemeal bread.

C-F: If asparagus is a new taste for children, you can involve them in its preparation, letting them snap off the asparagus stems at the bottom and mix the salad ingredients. You could always tell them what I tell children about broccoli – that they are giants and the asparagus tips are 'little people's' trees which are great to eat. It usually works!

Note: see page 227 for tips on for perfect hard-boiled eggs

VEGETABLE BIRYANI

Biryani is a classic Indian dish and it's cheap, versatile and really tasty. Cumin seeds give this biryani its authentic flavour, and don't stint on the onions, they are crucial in this recipe!

INGREDIENTS

340g (2 cups) of good quality basmati rice

300g (2 cups) frozen mixed vegetables, such as peas, beans, carrots

1 large potato in 2cm cubes

2 small peppers, 1 red and 1 green, deseeded and chopped in 2cm cubes

2 medium to large onions, finely chopped

1 large, ripe tomato, chopped

1 ½ tsp garam masala

½ tsp hot Madras curry powder

¼ tsp turmeric

½ tsp cumin seeds

2 tbsp oil

METHOD

1 Wash the rice in a strainer and leave to drain.

2 Bring 400ml (2 cups) of water to the boil in a saucepan, add a little salt and then the frozen vegetables. Bring back to the boil, remove from the heat and set aside.

3 Heat a frying pan, dry, and lightly toast the cumin seeds. Add 1 tbsp oil and then the chopped onions. Cook, stirring, on a high heat for a few minutes, until golden brown. Remove to a plate and add the other tbsp oil to the pan.

Heat until just beginning to smoke. Lightly brown the potatoes for a minute or so. Add the spices and stir, then add the tomato and peppers and season liberally with salt and black pepper.

4 Add the rest of the vegetables and the rice. Measure in 400ml (2 cups) of the cooking water, adding more water to bring it back to the required amount if necessary. Pour over the rice and vegetables. Bring to the boil and stir. Cover, and simmer on a very low heat for about 10 minutes, until the rice is cooked. Check seasoning and stir again. Turn off the heat and leave, covered, for another 10 minutes, and serve.

OPTIONS

Garnish with roasted cashews and serve with natural yoghurt and naan bread.

L: Omit the potato and reduce the oil to 1 tbsp.

C-F: Reduce the spices by half.

G-F: Check that the garam masala, curry powder and turmeric are gluten-free.

SHOPPING LIST
frozen mixed vegetables
red and green pepper
garam masala
cumin seeds

TOMATO SAUCE

This is a basic tomato sauce that can be used by itself with pasta or rice, or incorporated into other recipes. Don't be tempted to skimp on the onions, garlic or stock – the sauce just won't be the same.

INGREDIENTS

6 ripe, medium-sized tomatoes, chopped

2 x 400g can chopped tomatoes

6-8 large cloves of garlic, chopped finely

4 medium-sized onions, chopped finely

2 vegetable stock cubes

2 tbsp good quality olive oil or sunflower oil

1 level tbsp dried oregano

½ level tbsp dried basil

2 tbsp tomato purée

SHOPPING LIST
fresh tomatoes
tinned chopped tomatoes

METHOD

1 Heat the oil in a saucepan, and add the onions and garlic. The oil should be hot enough to make the onions and garlic sizzle but not brown. Cook, stirring frequently, until soft but still white. Add the fresh tomatoes and bring just to the boil, immediately turning the heat down to a simmer – you may need to take the pan off the heat for a minute or two to ensure it does not boil vigorously as this will make the tomatoes bitter.

2 Simmer for 20 minutes and then add the canned tomatoes, the stock cubes (dry) and the dried herbs. Bring just to the boil again and reduce the heat to a simmer. Simmer for 20 minutes or so and add the tomato purée. Remove from the heat and season with black pepper, and salt if necessary – the stock cubes may have added enough salt already.

3 If tomatoes are expensive, use two fresh tomatoes and three cans of chopped tomatoes instead of the tomato mix above.

4 On the other hand, if you just got a bonus, use good quality olive oil, one and a half times the quantity of fresh herbs to dried herbs and all fresh tomatoes – about 10-12.

5 And, of course, if you are seeking perfection, you could make your own stock and boil it down. (See page 229.)

OPTIONS

While hot stir in 200g chopped mozzarella cheese and 40g grated Parmesan cheese, and serve with pasta of your choice.

L: Serve with low-fat cheese.

G-F: Ensure the stock is gluten-free. Use gluten-free pasta.

TOFU & VEGETABLE STIR FRY

Tofu is a very healthy food but it can be bland. Here we marinate it to get some flavour in there, then add vegetables for a tasty stir fry. For help with stir frying, see page 229. (Firm tofu can be found in or near the cheese section of most supermarkets.)

INGREDIENTS

Tofu and marinade

250g firm tofu, approx., cut into strips 1cm wide and 5cm long

1 tbsp soy sauce

3-5 cloves of garlic, chopped finely

1 tbsp sunflower or corn oil

1 tsp toasted sesame oil

¼ tsp Szechuan pepper (you can get this in Asian shops, or you can substitute with normal pepper)

⅓ tsp sugar

Other ingredients

1-2 tbsp sunflower or corn oil

2-3 medium carrots, scraped, and cut into thin strips about 5cm long

1 large white onion, peeled and sliced into strips 1cm wide

3-4 broccoli florets sliced thinly

3 small peppers of different colours, washed and sliced into 1cm strips

100ml strong vegetable stock

½ tsp cornflour dissolved in 50ml (¼ cup) cold water

METHOD

1 Mix the tofu and marinade ingredients together and refrigerate for at least 30 minutes but not longer than 2 hours.

2 Heat 1 tbsp of oil in a wok or non-stick pan until it begins to smoke. Remove the tofu from the marinade and stir fry for approximately one minute on each side until golden. Remove from the pan and set aside.

3 Heat another tbsp of oil as above and stir fry the carrots and onions together for about 2 minutes. Add the peppers and broccoli and stir fry for one minute. Add the tofu and stir.

4 Mix together the tofu marinade, the dissolved cornflour and the vegetable stock and add to the pan. Stir all together quickly and remove from the heat. Taste and adjust seasoning if necessary.

OPTIONS

Serve with plain boiled rice and a little extra soy sauce if desired. (For how best to cook rice, see page 230.)

G-F: Ensure soy sauce, Szechuan pepper, sesame oil, stock and cornflour are gluten-free.

SHOPPING LIST
tofu, firm
carrots
broccoli
peppers
toasted sesame oil

COURGETTE & TOMATO GRATIN

This is a deliciously light, economical vegetarian dish which will serve four as a starter or two as a main course. Basically you scoop out the insides of the courgettes, mix them with some of the other ingredients and put them back in the skins, topping with cheese.

Oven 180°C/350°F/gas mark 4

INGREDIENTS

4 medium courgettes, washed

4 medium tomatoes, washed

2 large cloves of garlic, finely chopped

50g Parmesan or Cheddar cheese, grated

2 x 125g mozzarella balls

1 tsp dried basil or about 10 fresh basil leaves, chopped

2 tbsp olive/sunflower oil and a little more for brushing on the courgettes

SHOPPING LIST
courgettes
mozzarella balls
Cheddar or Parmesan
fresh basil, if not using dried

METHOD

1 Cut the courgettes in half, lengthways, and scoop out the centre. Brush lightly with oil and place, upside down, on a tray in the oven for 10 minutes.

2 Meanwhile chop the tomatoes and the insides of the courgettes and add to the chopped garlic and basil. Mix together with the rest of the oil and season with salt and black pepper.

3 Spoon this mixture into the courgettes. Sprinkle the Cheddar or Parmesan over and top with pieces of mozzarella.

4 Bake for about 40 minutes until golden on top.

OPTIONS

Serve with any or all of the following: green salad, crusty rolls, baked potato.

L: Use low-fat cheese.

G-F: Parmesan and mozzarella sometimes contain gluten so check the label. If you cannot find a gluten-free mozzarella, replace with a mild Cheddar cheese or a vegan mozzarella alternative.

GREEN PEA & PASTA SALAD

A bag of frozen peas is probably one of the most economical and versatile ways to feed a bunch of people. This is a fast, easy pasta and can be eaten straight away (I tend to eat it from the bowl as I make it) or refrigerated for later.

INGREDIENTS

500g (4 cups) frozen peas, cooked as directed on the packet and cooled

400g dried pasta

1 large red pepper, chopped into 1cm pieces

1 large onion, finely chopped

150ml (¾ cup) mayonnaise

2 tbsp white vinegar

1 tbsp sugar

2 tbsp milk

salt and black pepper

SHOPPING LIST

frozen peas
red pepper

METHOD

1 Cook pasta in boiling salted water until al dente. Drain, rinse under cold water and leave to drain again until cool.

2 In a large bowl, mix together the mayonnaise, vinegar, sugar and milk until smooth.

3 Add all the other ingredients, mix together well and season to taste.

OPTIONS

Serve on its own or with wholemeal bread, crusty rolls and/or a green salad.

L: Use light mayonnaise and low-fat milk.

G-F: Use gluten-free pasta and check that the mayonnaise and vinegar are gluten-free.

PUMPKIN & PEANUT CURRY

Pumpkin and peanut is a combination used on many continents. Africans use pumpkin leaves and peanuts together, Indians make pumpkin curry and here we have a Thai variation. The slightly sweet pumpkin, the heat from the chilli and the tangy lime make a delicious combination.

INGREDIENTS

500g approx. pumpkin, cut into 2cm squares (about 1kg unpeeled, unseeded pumpkin makes this amount)

1 large onion, finely sliced

1-2 green or red chillies, finely chopped

4-5 large cloves of garlic, crushed

2cm fresh ginger root, crushed (can be crushed with the garlic)

400ml can coconut milk

1½ tbsp sunflower or peanut oil

1 tbsp soy sauce or fish sauce

approx. 15g fresh coriander leaves, chopped

2 tbsp peanut butter

1 vegetable stock cube

zest and juice of 1 lime

½ tsp sugar

METHOD

1 Dissolve the stock cube in about 200ml (1 cup) boiling water and then add the peanut butter, stirring until it melts into the stock.

2 Heat oil in a large saucepan and cook the onions, stirring to prevent browning, until soft.

3 Add the garlic, ginger and chillies and cook for one minute, stirring all the time. Then add the pumpkin and cook, while stirring, for a couple of minutes.

4 Add all the other ingredients, leaving a few coriander leaves to sprinkle on top at the end. Stir, and simmer gently until the pumpkin is cooked but not mushy – around 15 minutes.

5 Season with salt and black pepper, garnish with some coriander leaves and serve.

OPTIONS

Serve with plain boiled rice, and extra soy sauce if desired.

L: Use low-fat coconut milk and low-fat peanut butter.

G-F: Use gluten-free stock and check that the soy or fish sauce is gluten-free.

SHOPPING LIST

pumpkin
ginger root
coconut milk
fresh coriander
peanut butter
lime
fish sauce, is using

CABBAGE & BEAN SOUP

Cabbage has so much good stuff in it – calcium for bones and teeth, magnesium for muscles and the nervous system, potassium and phosphorous for the heart and kidneys, and iodine, rarely found in vegetables, for the thyroid. And it is full of antioxidants for your skin and your liver. It's not only full of goodness and great value to buy, it's also delicious!

INGREDIENTS

half a head of green cabbage, washed and shredded

1 large onion, chopped

1 tbsp any oil except olive, for cooking the onions

3-4 cloves of garlic, peeled and chopped

2 large potatoes, peeled and cubed

600ml vegetable stock

1 tbsp oil of your choice: sunflower, corn, peanut

a knob of butter

1 tin broad beans in brine, drained and rinsed

salt

SHOPPING LIST

cabbage
tinned broad beans

METHOD

1 Heat 1 tbsp oil (not olive) in a large saucepan and cook the onions, without browning, until soft. Add the garlic, the cabbage and ¼ tsp salt and cook, stirring for a few minutes.

2 Add the stock and bring to the boil. Reduce the heat to a simmer.

3 Heat 1 tbsp oil and butter in a pan and fry the potato until golden. Add to the cabbage with the beans. Cover and simmer until cabbage and potato are cooked.

OPTIONS

Serve with garlic bread or bread of your choice.

L: Omit the potatoes.

G-F: Use gluten-free stock.

CARROT & PARSNIP GRATIN

Crunchy fresh vegetables combined with the nutty, sour taste of crème fraiche, the heat of mustard and, finally, topped with the deliciously mature taste of Parmesan – can life get any better?

Oven 190°C/375°F/gas mark 5

INGREDIENTS

500g carrots

500g parsnips

2 leeks

2 large potatoes

1 tbsp olive oil

400g crème fraiche

2 tsp mustard powder

½ tsp ground cinnamon or nutmeg

50g grated Parmesan

salt and pepper

a little butter

SHOPPING LIST

carrots
parsnips
leeks
potatoes
crème fraiche

METHOD

1 Peel and rinse, in cold water, the carrots, parsnips, potatoes and leeks. Cut into ½cm slices.

2 Bring a large pot of salted water to the boil and add the vegetables. Bring back to the boil and simmer for 3 minutes. Drain, allow to cool a little and mix in the tbsp olive oil.

3 Lightly butter an oven dish and add the vegetables.

4 Mix together the crème fraiche, mustard powder, cinnamon or nutmeg and some salt and pepper and pour mixture over the vegetables. Sprinkle with Parmesan and bake for 30-35 minutes.

OPTIONS

Serve with fresh, crusty bread. We often have it with hot buttered toast.

L: Omit the potatoes and use low-fat crème fraiche.

G-F: Ensure the mustard powder and Parmesan are gluten-free.

GREEN PEA CURRY

A curry is always very comforting. This variation is sweet and spicy with a little bit of a tang from the tomatoes.

INGREDIENTS

450g (3 cups) frozen peas

1 large potato, diced

3 ripe, medium-sized tomatoes, chopped

1 large onion, chopped

4 cloves of garlic, chopped

150ml vegetable stock

1 tsp ground cumin

½ tsp ground turmeric

½ tsp of a good quality, hot Madras curry powder

¼-½ tsp chilli powder, depending on how hot you like it

1 tbsp oil: corn, sunflower or peanut

salt to taste

SHOPPING LIST

frozen peas

METHOD

1 Heat the oil in a saucepan. Add the onions and cook, stirring from time to time, until golden brown. Add the garlic and stir. Add the spices and cook for a minute, being careful not to let the mixture burn.

2 Add the tomatoes and the stock and simmer for 5 minutes.

3 Add the potatoes and the frozen peas, bring to the boil and simmer for 5 minutes.

OPTIONS

Serve with boiled rice. A little natural yoghurt can be served on the side.

L: Leave out the potato.

C-F: Halve the spices and omit the chilli.

G-F: Make sure that the stock and spices are gluten-free.

LENTIL CURRY

Lentils are the ultimate shrewd food: cheap, nutritious and, when well cooked, really delicious. This curry includes potatoes and a little added tang from the tomato.

INGREDIENTS

100g red lentils

1 large onion, chopped

3 cloves of garlic, chopped

1 tbsp sunflower or corn oil

15g butter

½ tsp ground cumin

½ tsp turmeric

½ tsp of a good quality, hot Madras curry powder

½ tsp chilli powder (or more if preferred)

500ml vegetable stock

½ large, ripe tomato, chopped

2 medium-sized potatoes, cut into 1½cm cubes

SHOPPING LIST

red lentils

METHOD

1 Heat the oil and butter in a saucepan and add the onion and garlic. Cook, without browning, until they soften. Add the tomato and cook gently for a couple of minutes.

2 Add all the other ingredients, except the potatoes, bring to the boil and reduce the heat. Simmer for 5 minutes and then add the potatoes. Bring back to the boil and simmer, stirring occasionally, until the potatoes and lentils are cooked, approx. 15 mins.

OPTIONS

Serve with boiled basmati rice and/or naan or pitta bread.

L: Leave out the butter and the potatoes.

G-F: Ensure the stock and spices are gluten-free.

LEEK & PARMESAN RISOTTO

Risotto is at its best when just cooked, so I usually gather the troops before I start. The risk with this is that they get impatient, especially as the aroma of a simmering risotto begins to circulate, but it's better than having a delicious risotto go cold and sticky while rounding up the diners. The other thing to remember is to use a wooden spoon, as a metal one will break up the rice. And Fiona, a friend and wonderful home cook, and risotto aficionado, reckons that the secret of any good risotto is a glass of white wine, added towards the beginning, just after the first couple of spoonfuls of stock.

INGREDIENTS

2 leeks, trimmed, washed and cut into 1 cm rings

170g (1 cup) arborio rice

1 glass of white wine

1 litre hot vegetable stock

20g butter

2 tbsp grated Parmesan

SHOPPING LIST

leeks
white wine

METHOD

1 Melt the butter in a fairly large pan. Add the leeks and cook gently until they begin to soften – they need to retain a little firmness or they will go mushy as the rice is cooked.

2 Add the rice and stir until it's coated with the butter and heated well.

3 Stir in a couple of spoons of stock and let it simmer gently until the liquid has almost gone. Stir in the wine and repeat the process, letting the rice absorb the liquid and stirring from time to time.

4 Continue to add the stock, simmering gently and stirring frequently, until the rice is cooked – it needs to retain a little 'bite' so watch it towards the end, as you may not need all the stock.

5 Stir in the Parmesan and serve immediately.

OPTIONS

Serve with crusty bread or garlic bread and green salad.

L: Replace the butter with 1 tbsp olive oil.

G-F: Make sure the stock is gluten-free. If you cannot find gluten-free Parmesan replace with the same quantity of grated, extra mature Cheddar.

Note: *The possibilities for risotto are endless and it's a wonderful comfort food. In addition to the leeks try variations of one or more of the following: courgettes, red peppers, sun-dried tomatoes, peas, green beans, mushrooms.*

CABBAGE & LENTIL PIE

This is a healthy, nutritious and good value meal. I've used white rice here but brown rice can be used instead. It should be added at the same time as the lentils as it takes a while longer to cook than white rice.

Preheat grill to high

1 ovenproof pie dish approx. 22cm x 22cm x 5cm deep

INGREDIENTS

1 small to medium cabbage, washed and chopped

2 medium carrots, chopped

2 sticks of celery, chopped

1 large onion, chopped

3-4 cloves of garlic, chopped

1 tbsp oil of your choice

60g (⅓ cup) red lentils, washed

85g (½ cup) long grain rice, washed

300ml vegetable stock

a knob of butter to dress the cabbage and a little extra to grease the pie dish

1 mozzarella ball – 125g, or 150g grated Cheddar

salt and freshly ground black pepper

METHOD

1 Cook the cabbage in boiling salted water until tender. Drain and dress with a knob of butter and season with a little salt.

2 Heat the oil in a saucepan and add the carrots, celery, onion and garlic. Fry gently until soft. Add the lentils (and brown rice if using) and the stock and stir. Bring to a vigorous boil and stir.

3 Add the white rice if using. Bring to a vigorous boil and stir. Cover and reduce the heat to its lowest setting. Cook until the rice and lentils are soft, about 10-15 minutes. Stir carefully to separate the rice grains and add a little black pepper.

4 Mix the cabbage with the rice and lentils, and check the seasoning before placing the mixture in the lightly buttered pie dish. Dot with the mozzarella or sprinkle with the Cheddar. Place under a hot grill for about 5 minutes until golden on top. Serve hot.

OPTIONS

Serve with garlic bread, toast or potato wedges.

L: Leave out the butter and use low-fat mozzarella.

G-F: Use gluten-free stock. If you cannot find gluten-free mozzarella, use grated Cheddar cheese instead.

SHOPPING LIST
cabbage
carrots
celery
red lentils
mozzarella ball or Cheddar cheese

SHREWD
ENTERTAINING

I love having people over to dinner. Once the preparation is out of the way, it's an easy way of meeting up with friends – no driving therefore I can have a couple of glasses of wine, and at the end of the evening, when I'm tired, I don't have to face a journey to get to bed.

Some of the recipes in this section contain ingredients – especially steak, beef and lamb – that are normally expensive, but these are all regularly on special offer in supermarkets and, when they are, it's a great opportunity not only to stock the freezer but also to entertain in style.

Under the title of each menu is a suggestion for a starter and a dessert from the Shrewd Starters and Shrewd Desserts section.

TABLE DECORATING IDEAS

Table decorations can be done on a budget too and here are some suggestions that you may find useful.

* **GO WHITE**

   White is always chic, it goes with all colours and it never dates. A one-off investment in a good white linen tablecloth, with napkins to match, will serve you for many years and will always look good. Good quality white linen can be bleached and washed at the highest setting in your machine, which is great for getting stains out and keeping your linen snowy. Buy a simple white dinner set – they are very reasonably priced in many shops. Finish off with fresh white flowers and the barest amount of fresh green foliage – the effect on an all-white table is stunning. White lace curtains make inexpensive lace tablecloths.

* **USE WHAT YOU HAVE**

   If you have a beautiful wooden or glass table, display it. Use that crystal and the china that's a family heirloom – what good is there in having it if you can't enjoy it. Yes, it risks getting broken, but it will give you no joy while it's stored away.

* **USE A RUNNER**

   To add colour to your basic white or wooden table, use a runner. Instead of buying an expensive runner, buy a length of fabric, fold it double lengthwise and iron in folds it to hide the unhemmed sides. This not only gives definition to your table, but will help protect it from hot dishes and plates and provides a stage for your centrepiece and other table decorations.

* **USE LOTS OF CANDLES**

   Candles are inexpensive and give a lovely warm glow to a room. But never leave them alight in an empty room.

> **Note:** *When you sit down to eat, if you are short of space on the table for serving dishes etc., it's best to remove some of the table decorations, rather than have a crowded table. By then, the guests will have seen your table in all its glory and that all-important first impression will have been made.*

CENTREPIECES

Flowers are always good. If you have some in the garden, use them or use them to supplement those you buy. Buy flowers of one colour to match your table scheme.

* A centrepiece should be low or thin enough to allow guests to see each other across the table. Glass bowls of apples, lemons and limes, or indeed any fruit can be very pretty. Sticking to one type of fruit and one colour is more effective.

* A few loose pieces of fruit can be strewn around the bowl too. These decorations can be removed before the meal is served – their role is just to create that initial 'wow' factor.

* A staggered centrepiece of single flowers or candles in a row down the centre of the table or runner looks lovely.

* A bunch of hock glasses or champagne flutes, each one containing a single flower – an odd number is better – is very effective.

* A single centrepiece on a large table can look very lost – add smaller objects along the length of the table for balance.

* Use satin ribbons to tie around candle holders and vases. Make sure you buy real fabric ribbon, which is surprisingly inexpensive. You can tie ribbon around napkins too instead of napkin holders.

ENTERTAINING TIPS

* Plan the menu a few days in advance and make a list of everything you need, including aperitifs, wines and post-dinner drinks.

* Never use a recipe that you haven't cooked before – a dinner party is not the place to experiment.

* If possible, set the table the day before the event.

* Choose at least one course and, if possible, two that can be cooked or prepared in advance.

* Shop the day before – with the exception of seafood and fish which should be fresh on the day.

* Enjoy it – aim for perfection but laugh at glitches – you are probably the only person who will notice them anyway. A happy, relaxed host will make the guests feel relaxed too.

* No matter how frazzled you may be when the doorbell rings, greet your guests with a smile and make them feel welcome in your home – without people it's just bricks and mortar.

* A few stiff drinks before dinner – the guests, not you – makes everyone happy and hungry and the food will taste even more wonderful.

ROAST BEEF & ROAST POTATOES

Rib roast is the best for this recipe but a good quality housekeeper's cut can be used instead. Roast beef, especially rib, at normal price, is quite expensive but is very often on special offer in various supermarkets.

Suggested starter: **Mushroom & Leek Soup**

Suggested dessert: **Apple Crumble**

Oven 190°C/375°F/gas mark 5

INGREDIENTS

1-1¼ kg rib roast or housekeeper's cut

2 tbsp sunflower or corn oil

1 onion, sliced

10-12 small to medium potatoes

salt and freshly ground black pepper

SHOPPING LIST

rib roast or housekeeper's cut

METHOD

1 Heat 1 tbsp oil in a pan, or in the roasting dish if hob-safe, and sear the meat on all sides. Transfer to the roasting dish if using pan. Add the remaining oil and sprinkle the onion slices on top. Season with freshly ground black pepper and place in the oven.

2 Baste with the oil and juices every 15 minutes.

3 Cook for 45 minutes per kilo and 25 minutes over at the end, for rare to medium meat. Increase the time if you want it well done.

4 Meanwhile wash, peel and dry the potatoes. Place in the oven with the meat, about 35-45 minutes before the end of the cooking time, basting at first and then every 15 minutes, with the meat.

OPTIONS

Serve with vegetables of your choice and gravy.

L: Serve with a lightly dressed salad instead of potatoes.

C-F: Cook well and chop into small pieces to serve.

BAKED SEA BASS WITH THAI SAUCE

Sea bass is a lovely, juicy fish that soaks up flavours easily and keeps its shape. I love this simple Thai-inspired recipe, which can be prepared quickly and is full of flavour but still light. Fresh sea bass, even on offer, can be a little on the expensive side, but frozen, whole sea bass is usually reasonably priced and is often fresher than the 'fresh' counter.

Suggested starter: **Red Pepper Chicken Baskets**

Suggested dessert: **Orange Soufflés**

Oven 190°C/375°F/gas mark 5

INGREDIENTS

4 sea bass, gutted, whole or filleted

½ tbsp sunflower oil

salt

For the sauce

4 cloves of garlic

4cm fresh ginger root

1 red or green chilli

1 tbsp sesame oil

5 tbsp light soy sauce

½ tsp sugar

1 scallion, cut diagonally to serve

SHOPPING LIST

sea bass, whole or filleted
ginger root
sesame oil
scallion

METHOD

1 If the fish is whole, remove scales and fins. Wash fish and pat dry with kitchen paper.

2 Cut the whole fish diagonally down to the bone in two or three places on both sides. For the fillets, wash and pat dry with kitchen paper. Feel the fish for any bones not removed in filleting, and remove them with a tweezers.

3 Salt the fish, brush with oil and place on a lightly oiled, foil-covered oven tray. Bake for 25 minutes for the whole fish and 10-12 minutes for the fillets.

4 Crush the garlic, ginger and chilli together.

5 Heat the sesame oil in a saucepan and gently fry the garlic mixture for a minute or so. Add the soy sauce – it should sizzle a little – and then the sugar and cook gently for half a minute.

6 Remove the fish from the oven to hot plates and spoon the sauce over them. Sprinkle the scallions over each fish and serve.

OPTIONS

Serve with steamed rice and stir-fried vegetables, or new potatoes and green vegetables of your choice.

C-F: Remove the bones and skin and break the fish into small pieces.

G-F: Ensure the soy sauce is gluten-free.

PAN-FRIED ANGUS FILLET

Fillet steak is occasionally on special offer and, when it is, I like to buy in bulk and freeze. Simply cooked, this one is guaranteed to tantalise the taste buds.

Suggested starter: **Cream of Spinach Soup**

Suggested dessert: **Poires Belle Hélène**

INGREDIENTS

4 slices of fillet beef (400-600g total weight)

1 large onion, sliced

2 tbsp sunflower, corn or peanut oil

30g butter

salt and freshly ground black pepper

SHOPPING LIST

fillet beef

METHOD

1 Remove beef from the fridge about 20 minutes before cooking. Just before placing on the pan, season the beef lightly with salt and freshly ground black pepper.

2 Heat 1 tbsp oil in a pan until hot but not smoking. Add half the butter and then the onions. Sauté for a couple of minutes until golden but still firm. Remove to a heated dish and keep warm.

3 Wipe the pan with kitchen paper and add the other tbsp oil. Heat until just beginning to smoke. Add the steaks and sear on high for one minute each side. Reduce the heat and cook as follows:

Rare
1½ minutes more each side.

Medium
2½ minutes more each side.

Well done
3½ minutes more each side.

Just before you remove from the pan, add the rest of the butter.

5 Transfer to a heated plate and rest for 5 minutes before serving.

OPTIONS

Serve with new potatoes and vegetables of your choice, or a simple green salad. Also delicious with ratatouille (see page 142).

L: Omit the butter.

C-F: Cook well and chop into small pieces to serve.

CHICKEN & MIXED VEGETABLE PIE

A Western diet typically contains too much meat and not enough vegetables, and this pie is one of my many attempts to address that. I've simply reduced the amount of meat one would normally use and increased the vegetable content. I often have this when I have friends over as it can be partly prepared ahead to Stage 3, and refrigerated for later use.

Suggested starter: **Stuffed Garlic Mushrooms**

Suggested dessert: **Plum Cobbler**

Heat grill to hot

Ceramic oven dish, approx. 30cm x 20cm x 5cm deep

INGREDIENTS

500g boneless chicken breast

2 medium carrots, chopped into small squares

1 stick of celery, chopped

1 large onion, sliced

450ml strong chicken stock

¾ glass of white wine

3 tbsp crème fraiche

500g broccoli, cut into small florets

about 8 medium potatoes

100ml (½ cup) milk

30g butter

salt and freshly ground black pepper

METHOD

1 Peel and halve the potatoes and bring to the boil in salted water. Simmer until tender. Drain, add the milk and mash into the potatoes. Then mix in the butter, and season with salt.

2 Turn the oven on to its lowest setting.

3 While the potatoes are cooking cut the chicken into slices about 2cm x 1cm. Put them into a saucepan with the stock, celery, onion and carrots, and bring to the boil. Immediately reduce the heat and simmer gently, until cooked – 10-15 minutes. I like mine a bit on the crunchy side but this is a matter of personal taste, however the chicken must be cooked through. With a slotted spoon, remove the chicken and vegetables to a lightly buttered oven dish, and keep warm in the oven.

(At this stage you can cool the chicken and vegetables and refrigerate for use later in the day or the next day.)

4 Add the broccoli to the stock and bring to the boil. Reduce the heat immediately and simmer gently for 3-4 minutes. Remove from the stock with a slotted spoon. Set aside and keep warm.

5 Add the wine to the stock and boil rapidly until the liquid reduces by two thirds. Stir in the crème fraiche. Pour the sauce over the chicken and vegetables in the oven dish, and then layer the broccoli on top. Dot the mashed potato on top and spread out with a fork until covered.

6 Place under the grill until golden brown. Serve immediately.

OPTIONS

This is a complete meal in itself, but I usually serve it with extra green vegetables such as mangetout or spinach.

L: Use half-fat crème fraiche and don't add any butter to the potatoes.

G-F: Ensure stock is gluten-free stock

SHOPPING LIST
chicken breast fillets
carrots
celery
crème fraiche
broccoli

MARINATED FRIED SIRLOIN

Sirloin steak is regularly on special offer in supermarkets and I always use the opportunity to stock up the freezer. There are many ways to ensure that your steak is tender and juicy. Here we will look at two of them, namely salting it and marinating it.

Suggested starter: **Cauliflower Soup**

Suggested dessert: **Old-Fashioned Irish Apple Tart**

INGREDIENTS

800g-1kg sirloin steak, about 2cm thick, cut into 4 portions

sunflower or corn oil for frying

a generous knob of butter

For the salting method

preferably rock or sea salt

For the marinade

3 tbsp soy sauce

3 cloves of garlic, peeled and crushed

2 tbsp sunflower or corn oil

salt and freshly ground black pepper

SHOPPING LIST

sirloin steak
salad, to serve with steak

METHOD

1: SALTING

1 Liberally coat both sides of the meat with sea salt and leave at room temperature for about 20-30 minutes. Rinse off the salt, thoroughly, and pat very dry with kitchen paper.

2 Heat oil in a heavy-based pan until it begins to smoke and add the steak. Sear each side for about one minute. Then turn the heat down slightly and cook as follows:

Rare
cook for a further ½-1 minute each side.

Medium
cook for a further 1-1½ minutes each side.

Well done
cook for a further 1½-2 minutes each side.

3 Just before finishing, add a generous knob of butter – optional but very, very good!

4 Transfer to a warm plate and allow to rest for five minutes before serving.

METHOD 2: MARINATING

1 Mix the marinade ingredients, and coat steak with the mix. Refrigerate and leave for at least 30 minutes, but preferably overnight.

2 Remove steak from marinade, pat dry and cook as for Method 1 above.

3 Remove from the pan to a warmed plate. Add marinade to the pan. Bring to the boil and pour over the steak.

OPTIONS

Serve with one or any combination of the following: baked, mashed potato or chips/wedges, salad of your choice.

L: Trim the steak of any fat. Don't add butter at the end and serve with a plain salad with low-fat dressing.

C-F: Cook well and chop into small pieces to serve.

G-F: Ensure the soy sauce is gluten-free.

CHICKEN CHASSEUR

This classic French dish is tangy and tastes sublime. It is also easy and fast to prepare, and can be an any day treat or served at a dinner party.

Suggested starter: **Fresh Tomato Soup**

Suggested dessert: **Chocolate Brownies**

INGREDIENTS

8 chicken oyster thighs or drumsticks (4 breasts for the leaner version)

3-4 large cloves of garlic, chopped

1 medium onion, finely chopped

200g mushrooms, preferably large, cleaned and chopped roughly

3 ripe medium-sized tomatoes, chopped

200ml (1¾ glases) white wine

1 tbsp fresh parsley, chopped

100ml strong chicken stock

1 tbsp oil

50g butter

salt and white pepper

SHOPPING LIST

chicken thighs/drumsticks or breasts if using the leaner version
mushrooms
fresh parsley

METHOD

1 Heat oil in a pan until hot but not smoking. Add the chicken, skin side down. Season liberally with salt and black pepper. Cook for about 2 minutes until golden and then turn and cook on the other side for about 2 minutes more. Remove from the pan to a heated plate.

2 Add the butter to the pan and then the mushrooms. Sauté until a little golden and then add the onions. Sauté for about 2 minutes together and then add the garlic, chicken and the stock. Bring to the boil, cover and simmer for 35-40 minutes until the chicken is cooked through.

3 Remove the chicken again and keep warm. Add the wine to the sauce and cook until the sauce is reduced by about a half. Add the tomatoes and allow to simmer for a couple of minutes before stirring in the parsley. Check seasoning and serve the chicken with the sauce poured over it.

OPTIONS

Serve with gratin dauphinois (no cheese) and any green vegetable of your choice.

L: Use chicken breast fillets instead of oyster thighs or drumsticks. Chop the fillets into four or five pieces. Replace the butter with 2 tbsp olive oil.

G-F: Ensure stock is gluten-free.

SIRLOIN WITH STILTON

My first foray into the big world helped develop my taste for good food. I worked for a few school holidays, as a waitress, in a yacht club in Dun Laoghaire. This was an introduction to Irish fine dining at its best. I can remember standing at the dumb waiter, with my back to the diners, eating buttered digestives, heaped with Stilton from a freshly arrived block, and hoping I wouldn't get caught. I love Stilton when it's fresh on sweet, buttered biscuits, and then when it gets a bit strong, I make a sauce. This is a very simple sauce and can be rustled up in a few minutes, and it's perfect with steak.

Suggested starter: **Asparagus & Lemon Soup**

Suggested dessert: **Tarte Tatin aux Pommes**

INGREDIENTS

1-1¼kg steak – sirloin, fillet or any good quality frying steak

250g mushrooms, cleaned and sliced

2 tbsp sunflower or corn oil

250ml cream

100g Stilton cheese

½ tsp sugar

salt and freshly ground black pepper

SHOPPING LIST

steak
mushrooms
Stilton
cream

METHOD

1 Salt steak generously and leave at room temperature for 15 minutes.

2 Turn the oven to the lowest setting, to heat the plates and to have a warm place for the steak to rest.

3 Wash the steak under cold water and pat dry with kitchen paper.

4 Heat 1 tbsp of oil in a frying pan until it starts to smoke and sear the steak for one minute on each side. Continue to cook according to taste as follows:

Rare
cook for a further ½-1 minute each side.

Medium
cook for a further 1-1½ minutes each side.

Well done
cook for a further 1½-2 minutes each side.

5 Place the steak on a warm plate in the oven and wipe the pan with kitchen paper.

6 Heat the other tbsp of oil in the same pan and stir fry the mushrooms for 3-4 minutes, until slightly golden. Add the cream and the sugar, and then crumble in the Stilton (including the rind). Heat gently, stirring, until the cheese melts into the cream – do not boil. Season with a little salt (the cheese is already somewhat salty so it doesn't need much) and some black pepper, and spoon the sauce over the steak. Serve immediately.

OPTIONS

Serve with baked potatoes and vegetables.

L: Enjoy and start again tomorrow!

C-F: Stilton may be a somewhat strong taste for children, so the children's portion(s) of sauce may be removed before adding the Stilton. In this case, reduce the amount of Stilton added to ensure the flavours balance.

G-F: There would appear to be contradictory theories as to whether Stilton contains gluten or not. If in doubt, replace with a mature Cheddar.

TROUT EN PAPILLOTE

This classic French method of cooking fish is simple and fast. The finished product will be light and full of flavour and look very impressive.

Suggested starter: **Butternut Squash Soup**

Suggested dessert: **Meringue-Topped Tapioca Pudding**

Oven 170°C/340°F/gas mark 3½

INGREDIENTS

4 trout, scaled, filleted and divided into 2 pieces

40g butter

1 tbsp chopped fresh parsley and the leaves from a couple of sprigs of thyme

salt and pepper

a little extra butter for the foil

Tin foil to wrap up the fish for cooking

SHOPPING LIST

trout

fresh parsley

fresh thyme (or dried)

METHOD

1 Feel the fish, gently, for any stray bones and remove them with tweezers.

2 Cut four squares of tinfoil, big enough to fold over the fish and with spare foil to seal the packets. Smear the foil with a little butter.

3 Mix the butter with the herbs and salt and pepper to taste.

4 Spread the butter onto the flesh side of the fillets and sandwich together in twos. Place each sandwich onto a piece of foil and fold the foil over the fish, sealing tightly.

5 Place on a baking tray in the preheated oven and bake for about 20 minutes, until the fish is just tender. Serve immediately.

OPTIONS

Serve with steamed tender spring vegetables such as asparagus, or carrots and peas, and steamed, buttered new potatoes.

L: Replace the butter with olive oil and a squeeze of lemon juice.

C-F: Make sure all bones have been removed from the fish. I've found that children like the idea of dinner in a parcel.

COLD WHOLE SALMON SALAD

Salmon, at the tail end of the season, is big, fat and excellent value for money. You will need a large saucepan, a salmon dish or a big serving dish, and half a dozen people with a large appetite. Have the fish gutted and descaled before you buy it, as it's a very dirty job to do at home. Cook it the night before for lunch or early in the morning for dinner.

Suggested starter: **Pan-Seared Aubergine with Mozzarella**

Suggested dessert: **Caramelised Fresh Fruit**

INGREDIENTS

1 large, whole salmon, gutted and descaled

2 vegetable stock cubes

cucumber and mayonnaise to serve

SHOPPING LIST

1 whole salmon

cucumber to serve

METHOD

1 Wash fish and coil in a large saucepan. Cover with cold water, add the stock cubes and cover with a lid.

2 Bring to the boil and remove from the heat. Leave to cool for several hours or overnight.

3 Prepare a large dish with salad.

4 Remove the fish carefully from the saucepan to the serving plate. If you wish you can remove the head, and the skin from the uppermost side, and decorate with slices of cucumber, or just serve whole.

OPTIONS

Serve with salad and homemade brown soda bread or other wholewheat bread. Potato salad, or sautéed or chipped potatoes are also delicious with the salmon, and a good quality mayonnaise is essential.

L: Use a low-fat mayonnaise to serve.

G-F: Use gluten-free stock and mayonnaise.

STEAK & CARAMELISED ONIONS

The cold weather can bring out the carnivore in me, and then there's nothing to beat good, old-fashioned steak and onions.

Suggested starter: **Citrus Sardine Salads on Blinis**

Suggested dessert: **Fresh Fruit Salad**

INGREDIENTS

About 1kg of steak, sirloin, fillet or any good quality steak

1 tbsp oil for frying

2-3 large red or white onions, sliced

1 tbsp brown sugar

1 tbsp sunflower or corn oil

1 tbsp balsamic vinegar

1 tbsp butter

Rock or sea salt

black pepper

SHOPPING LIST

steak

balsamic vinegar

METHOD

1 Salt the steak generously on both sides and leave to sit, at room temperature, for 15 minutes.

2 Meanwhile, heat the oil and butter in a frying pan and add the onions. Cook gently for about 15 minutes, until golden, stirring occasionally. It's important that the onions cook slowly and do not brown.

3 When the onions are soft, add the brown sugar and a little salt. Cook uncovered, over a medium heat, stirring all the time, until the onions are golden brown and caramelised.

4 Rinse the salt from the steak, under the cold water tap, and pat very dry with kitchen paper.

5 In a separate, heavy pan, heat the oil until smoking, and cook the steak for one minute on each side. Then reduce the heat a little, and cook as follows:

Rare
cook for a further ½-1 minute each side.

Medium
cook for a further 1-1½ minutes each side.

Well done
cook for a further 1½-2 minutes each side.

> **Note:** *if using fillet steak, it's normally thicker so will need a little extra cooking time.*

6 Transfer to a warmed plate and allow to rest for about 5 minutes before serving.

7 Reheat the onion, add the vinegar and serve immediately with the steak.

OPTIONS

Serve with baked potatoes and butter.

L: Have the steak and half a portion of onions, with a plain salad.

C-F: Cook well and chop into small pieces.

GIGOT À LA CUILLÈRE

This is a very easy, economical French recipe. Basically you brown the lamb chops, throw in the rest of the ingredients and cook it in the oven. The French sometimes call it Gigot de Sept Heures or Seven Hour Gigot because they cook it in the oven for seven hours – a great idea if you are going to be out most of the day and want dinner ready when you get home. It can also be cooked faster though. If you are having guests for dinner, the delicious aroma of the food will greet them at the door.

Suggested starter: **Red Kidney Bean Soup**

Suggested dessert: **Cranberry Pineapple**

Oven: Slow method, preheat to 120˚C/250˚F/gas mark ½

Fast method, preheat to 160˚C/310˚F/gas mark 2½

INGREDIENTS

4 good-sized gigot lamb chops

1 large onion, sliced

1 leek, washed and chopped into 2cm rounds

2 medium carrots, chopped into 2cm rounds

100ml (1 glass) white wine

100ml chicken or vegetable stock

bay leaf

fresh thyme

1 tbsp sunflower, corn or peanut oil

salt and black pepper

METHOD

Season the lamb well with salt and pepper. Heat oil in a pan until smoking and brown the meat on both sides. Add the stock, herbs, wine and the vegetables and bring to the boil. Transfer to an ovenproof casserole dish and cover.

2 Cook for 3 hours at 160°C for the fast method and 7 hours at 120°C for the slow method. If you have time, the slow method is better as the flavour will improve and the meat will be deliciously tender.

3 If you want a thicker sauce, strain the cooking liquid into a saucepan and boil rapidly until it reduces.

OPTIONS

Serve with mashed potatoes or steamed new potatoes. It's also delicious with crusty bread.

L: Trim the lamb chops of all fat and gristle.

G-F: Ensure stock is gluten-free.

SHOPPING LIST
gigot lamb chops
leek
carrots
fresh thyme

GREEK ROAST LAMB

Entertaining is an important feature of Cypriot life, and this one of the great ways that they cook a roast of lamb. If you have time, prepare the lamb and leave in the fridge for a few hours or overnight, for the flavours to spread through the meat. This is a good dinner party dish as it can be prepared for roasting the day before. While it's cooking there's plenty of time to work on the accompaniments and the other courses, with time to spare to sip a glass of wine with your guests.

Starter: **Pancetta Frutada**

Dessert: Irish Whiskey Baked Apples with Cream

Oven 240°C/475°F/gas mark 9

INGREDIENTS

shoulder or leg of lamb (on the bone) about 1-1¼kg

3-4 large cloves of garlic, cut lengthways into 2-3 slices

6-8 large potatoes

2 tbsp oil of your choice

½ tsp dried rosemary, thyme or oregano

1 onion, sliced

1 lemon, quartered

¾ tsp salt

black pepper

SHOPPING LIST

shoulder or leg of lamb on the bone

METHOD

1 Make slits in the meat with a sharp knife and insert a slice of garlic into each one. Season the meat with herbs, salt and black pepper. Coat with 1 tbsp oil and a little lemon juice from one of the lemon quarters and put into a roasting pan, along with the onion and lemon quarters. Cover the onion and lemon quarters with foil. Place in the preheated oven and cook for 30 minutes, basting after 15 minutes.

2 Reduce the heat to 125°C/250°F/gas mark ½ and cover with tinfoil. Cook for a further 3 hours.

3 Meanwhile peel the potatoes and cut them in half. Rinse them with cold water and pat dry with kitchen paper. Season liberally with salt and black pepper and coat with the remaining tbsp oil.

4 Remove the lamb from the oven dish to a warmed oven tray, cover with foil and keep warm.

5 Turn up the oven to 240°C/475°F/gas mark 9. Pour off a little of the fat from the meat juices, add the potatoes and baste. Cook for about 45 minutes, basting every 15 minutes. Twenty minutes before the end, return the lamb to the oven to brown.

OPTIONS

Great served with a lemony Greek salad or blanched mangetout.

L: Trim the lamb of any fat and leave out the potatoes altogether. Reduce the oil to 1 tbsp.

RIB EYE & RED WINE SAUCE

This is a rich sauce that goes extremely well with steak. If you have it with a glass or two of red wine, you don't need to worry so much about the butter.

Suggested starter: **Thai Lobster Salad**

Suggested dessert: **Fresh Fruit Salad**

INGREDIENTS

800g-1kg rib eye steak

about 2tbsp oil for frying the steak

coarsely ground rock salt

For the Sauce

100g butter

1 large onion, finely chopped

½ glass of red wine, preferably dry

110ml extra strong chicken stock

1 tsp Dijon mustard

salt and freshly ground black pepper

SHOPPING LIST

rib eye steak
Dijon mustard

METHOD

1 Remove the steak from the fridge and salt liberally on both sides, with rock salt, and set aside.

2 Meanwhile, heat one third of the butter in a large saucepan and add the chopped onions. Fry gently until they have softened. Add the wine and the stock and simmer until the liquid has reduced by half. Add the remainder of the butter and the mustard and whisk well. Taste and season if necessary.

3 Wash the salt off the steaks and pat dry with kitchen towel.

4 Heat the oil until smoking and add the steak. Fry for one minute on each side and reduce the heat a little and continue to cook as preferred as follows:

Rare
cook for a further ½-1 minute each side.

Medium
cook for a further 1-1½ minutes each side.

Well done
cook for a further 1½-2 minutes each side.

OPTIONS

Serve with new potatoes and vegetables of your choice.

L: Omit the butter.

C-F: Serve the children's portion(s) chopped in small pieces and with only a little sauce.

G-F: Use gluten-free stock and if gluten-free Dijon mustard is not available, replace with 1 tsp of English mustard dissolved in 1 tsp gluten-free, white, distilled vinegar.

SHREWD
DESSERTS

A lot of the desserts that I make are tried and tested, traditional. They hark back to times when people, including myself, had a lot less money to spend.

For reasons of health and economy, a lot have fruit as the main ingredient. I make these when the particular fruit is in season and the prices are very low. When looking for low-priced seasonal fruit, I often find that green-grocers as well as supermarkets have very good value.

APPLE CRUMBLE

Normally I would make an apple crumble from Bramley apples, but when they are not in season I use eating apples and add some lemon juice for a bit of bite. I've included a gluten-free topping variation.

Oven 190°C/375°F/gas mark 5

INGREDIENTS

6 Bramley or other green cooking apples

2 tbsp sugar

For the crumble

115g plain flour

80g oat flakes

85g butter

115g demerara/brown sugar

For the gluten-free crumble

45g of Tritamyl gluten-free flour

60g (⅔ cup) of dessicated coconut

2 tbsp brown sugar

50g butter

SHOPPING LIST

cooking apples, preferably Bramleys
oat flakes
Tritamyl gluten-free flour, if using
dessicated coconut, if using

METHOD

1 Put all the crumble ingredients together in a bowl. Rub the butter in with your fingers.

2 Peel, core and slice the apples and put in a buttered oven dish. Add the sugar.

3 Cover with the crumble mixture and place in the oven.

4 Bake for about 45 minutes until golden on top.

OPTIONS

Serve with ice cream and/or cream. Also very good with custard.

L: Reduce the butter to 70g, or 40g for the gluten-free variation.

G-F: Use the gluten-free topping and proceed as above.

JELLIED ORANGES

This is a bit of a kiddie dessert but I've seen many an adult tuck into one. They are very colourful and a plateful of these are great for a summer party.

INGREDIENTS

4 large oranges

1 packet of green jelly

1 packet of red jelly

green fruit such as grapes or kiwifruit (8-10 seedless green grapes, halved, or 1 ripe kiwi, peeled and cut into chunks)

red fruit such as strawberries (4 quartered) or cherries (8 halved) or raspberries (8 halved)

SHOPPING LIST

oranges, large
jelly, green and red
kiwi or green seedless green grapes
strawberries, raspberries or cherries

METHOD

1 Wash the oranges and cut them in half. Cut out the flesh, being careful not to break the skin. The flesh and juice is not necessary for the recipe so it can be refrigerated for later use – perfect to use in the Clementine Clafoutis, which follows.

2 Make the red jelly with hot water as usual, using half the amount of water on the packet instructions.

3 Wash and dry the fruit and add some of the red fruit to half of the orange skins. Pour in the jelly to fill the skins.

4 Repeat the process with the green jelly and green fruit, using the remaining half of the orange skins.

5 Leave the jelly to set and then cut each jellied orange carefully in half. Arrange four of the pieces of jellied orange on each plate.

OPTIONS

Serve with some fresh cream or ice-cream.

L: Omit the cream and ice-cream.

CLEMENTINE CLAFOUTIS

This dish can be made with clementines, and most types of oranges. As this is best warm and doesn't really keep, you just have to eat it all! The amount of fruit can increased or decreased to taste.

Oven 170°C/340°F/gas mark 3½

Oven dish 28cm x 18cm x 5cm deep, approx.

INGREDIENTS

8-12 clementines or 4-5 oranges, peeled and separated into segments (if using oranges, halve each segment)

a little butter for the oven dish

3 eggs, at room temperature

1 pinch of salt

200g (1 cup sugar)

150ml (¾ cup) cream

150ml (¾ cup) milk

65g (½ cup) flour and a little extra for the oven dish

1 tsp vanilla essence

a little icing sugar to dust the top

SHOPPING LIST

clementines or oranges

cream

METHOD

1 Butter the oven dish and dust it with a little flour. Scatter the clementine segments over the bottom of the dish.

2 Put the eggs into a bowl with a pinch of salt and whisk until frothy. Whisk in the sugar and vanilla very quickly followed by the cream and milk. Fold in the flour quickly and gently, and pour the batter over the clementines.

3 Bake in the preheated oven for 40-45 minutes until golden brown on top. To check that it is done, insert a skewer or small knife, and if it comes out clean, the clafoutis is cooked.

4 Dust with icing sugar and serve hot.

OPTIONS

Serve on its own or with a little fresh cream or ice-cream.

G-F: Replace the flour with gluten-free flour.

CHOCOLATE BROWNIES

Lorrie, an American friend who lives in Dubai, gave me this brownie recipe. When it comes to cakes and cookies, Lorrie is one of the best cooks I know. We had many a long chat over food and swapped a lot of recipes, and this is one of her best.

Oven 180°C/350°F/gas mark 4

Oven dish 20cm x 18cm x 5cm deep, approx.

INGREDIENTS

95g (¾ cup) flour

80g (¾ cup) cocoa

140g melted butter

300g (1½ cups) sugar (ordinary granulated, not caster sugar)

1 heaped tsp powdered instant coffee

3 large free-range eggs, beaten

1½ tsp vanilla extract

½ tsp salt

SHOPPING LIST

cocoa
instant coffee powder

METHOD

1 Generously butter the oven dish.

2 Combine the flour, cocoa and salt in one bowl.

3 Whisk butter and coffee in another bowl. Add the sugar, whisking to blend. Add the eggs, one at a time, whisking well after each one, and then whisk in the vanilla.

4 Add the flour mix, whisking until just blended – it's important not to over-mix here.

5 Spoon the mixture into the prepared oven dish and bake for 35-40 minutes until a skewer or a thin knitting needle inserted in the middle comes out clean. Don't over-bake – brownies are supposed to be a bit squidgy in the middle.

OPTIONS

Serve warm with cream or vanilla ice cream. Can also be served cold.

L: Replace the butter with low-fat spread, and leave out the cream or ice cream.

G-F: Replace the flour with the same quantity of Tritamyl gluten free flour and make as above. The gluten-free version may take 5 or 10 minutes longer to bake than the gluten version, but be careful not to over-bake. Serve as above.

ORANGE SOUFFLÉS

In terms of timing, this is the perfect dessert for me, as I rarely want a dessert immediately after eating a starter and a main course. Soufflés really need to be made and baked after the main course is eaten (unless you want to be slaving away in the kitchen while everyone else is eating), as they have to be eaten right away, before they begin to go flat, so there will be a time lapse between the main course and the dessert. However, if everything is measured out in advance, they take only about 10 minutes to prepare.

Oven to 190°C/375°F/gas mark 5

4 small ramekin dishes of 175ml capacity

INGREDIENTS

25g flour, plus extra for the ramekin dishes

2 eggs, at room temperature

½ tsp vanilla essence

juice and grated peel of half a large, unwaxed orange

30g butter and extra for buttering the ramekin dishes

125ml milk

60g caster sugar

a pinch of salt

a little icing sugar to serve (optional)

SHOPPING LIST

large unwaxed orange

METHOD

1 Generously butter (and it has to be generous or the soufflés will stick – use butter from the fridge for a thicker coating) four small ramekin dishes and dust lightly with flour.

2 Separate the egg yolks and whites. Place the whites in a bowl, add a pinch of salt and beat them until the foam forms stiff peaks but is still glossy. Set aside.

3 Melt the butter in a saucepan until it just starts foaming, add the orange peel and the flour and cook, stirring, for 2 minutes on a low heat. Add the milk in about four separate amounts, and whisk constantly, allowing the sauce to thicken after each addition. Remove the saucepan from the heat and stir in the sugar, the orange juice, vanilla and the egg yolks.

4 Carefully fold in the egg whites (don't over-mix, you can ignore small bits of egg white not mixed in) and divide the mixture between the ramekins, making sure that they are no more than three-quarters full.

5 Bake in the preheated oven for about 15 minutes. To check if it's done, shake the ramekin a little – the soufflé should have a slight wobble. The perfect soufflé has a centre that is a little gooey. Dust with a little icing sugar and serve immediately.

6 Note: Soufflés start to sink the minute they come out of the oven, so they need to be taken straight to the table.

OPTIONS

The soufflés are eaten on their own, straight away.

L: Use low-fat milk.

G-F: Use the same quantity of gluten-free Tritamyl flour in place of normal flour and make as above. This recipe adapts perfectly to the gluten-free version.

> **Note:** *One of the secrets of a successful soufflé is for eggs to be room temperature.*

RICE PUDDING WITH CARAMELISED APPLES

I was reared on desserts like rice pudding, sago and semolina and I still love them. They have largely gone out of fashion and it's such a pity because, apart from being delicious, they are both economical and nutritious. This is a recipe for rice pudding with a succulent centre of caramelised apples. It can be eaten hot or cold and either way, it's very, very good.

Oven 165°C/325°F/gas mark 3

Oven dish 30cm x 20cm x 5cm deep, approx.

INGREDIENTS

For the rice

100g (just over half cup) pudding rice

1 litre milk

a little butter to grease the oven dish

1 egg, beaten

a pinch of cinnamon powder

2-3 tbsp sugar

For the apples

4 firm, cooking apples

100g (just over half cup) sugar

40g butter

SHOPPING LIST

cooking apples, preferably Bramleys

METHOD

1 Wash the rice in cold water and drain. Place into a saucepan with the milk and cinnamon and bring to the boil. Reduce the heat and simmer very, very gently until soft – this can take up to an hour. Sweeten to taste with the sugar. Allow to cool a little.

2 Meanwhile, peel, core and slice the apples. Melt the butter and sugar in a large saucepan. Put in the apples and cook on high, stirring frequently but being careful not to break the apples, until dark golden brown and caramelised – this will take about 5 minutes.

3 Generously butter your oven dish.

4 Just before you are about to put it into the oven, mix the beaten egg into the warm rice. Spoon half the mixture into the oven dish. Layer the caramelised apples over the rice (if they have gone hard, put the pot back on the hob and heat a little until the caramel is pliable again) and top with the remainder of the rice.

5 Bake for about 35 minutes until the top of the rice is golden. If necessary finish off under the grill to turn the top a golden brown. Can be served hot or cold.

OPTIONS

This is delicious on its own but a little fresh pouring or whipped cream may be served with it.

Other fresh fruits can be substituted for apples, e.g. peaches, plums, nectarines, pears. Jams and conserves can be used too, and my favourite is a few tablespoons of a good strawberry jam.

L: Use low-fat milk and serve without cream.

G-F: Use gluten-free cinnamon powder or use a little freshly grated nutmeg instead.

Note on caramellising the apples:

When the apples start to change colour, watch them carefully as they can burn very easily. At this point they will smell divine, they will look amazing and your instinct will be to put the spoon in your mouth – don't – caramel reaches an extremely high temperature and you run the risk of being burned. Set aside until the rice is done.

IRISH WHISKEY BAKED APPLES & WHIPPED CREAM

This is a very traditional dessert for wintertime, and one that we tend to forget about. I like to have the apples slightly overcooked and fluffy. Served with slightly sweetened whipped cream, this is a dessert fit for royalty.

Oven 170°C/340°F/gas mark 3½

INGREDIENTS

4 Bramley apples

145g (⅔ cup) brown sugar

75g (½ cup) raisins

50ml (¼ cup) Irish whiskey

1 tbsp lemon juice

¼ tsp cinnamon powder

grating of fresh nutmeg

1 tbsp butter

500ml cream

1½ tbsp caster sugar

a little icing sugar to sprinkle on top when cooked

SHOPPING LIST

cooking apples, preferably Bramleys
raisins
Irish whiskey
cream

METHOD

1 Soak the raisins in the whiskey overnight. Then add the sugar, lemon, cinnamon and nutmeg.

2 Line an oven tray with aluminium foil.

3 Wash and core the apples. Stuff with the raisin mixture, adding a little butter to each apple, and place on the oven tray.

4 Bake for 30-45 minutes, until
tender all the way through,
basting once or twice with the
syrup.

5 Add the sugar to the cream and
whip until stiff.

OPTIONS

Place an apple and a little mound of
whipped cream on a large plate. Top
the cream with one or two of the
stray raisins, and sprinkle the whole
plate with icing sugar.

L: Leave out the butter and serve
with a little low-fat, slightly sweetened
yoghurt or cottage cheese instead of
cream.

C-F: Use eating apples and do not
soak the raisins in whiskey.

G-F: Use gluten-free cinnamon
powder or leave out altogether.
Ensure that icing sugar used is gluten-
free.

Note: *The raisins need to be
soaked in the whiskey overnight,
so forward planning is needed.*

PLUM COBBLER

We have, I believe, the Americans to thank for fruit cobblers. They come in all shapes and sizes and this one is a very fast and easy dessert. The plums can be replaced with other fruits, either tinned or fresh.

Oven 160°C/310°F/gas mark 2½

Oven dish 28cm x 20cm x 5cm deep, approx.

INGREDIENTS

6 plums, halved and stoned

130g (1 cup)flour

200g (1 cup) sugar

55g butter

150ml (¾ cup) milk

1 egg (room temperature) beaten

2 tsp baking powder

SHOPPING LIST

fresh plums

METHOD

1 To make the batter, put the flour, egg, sugar, baking powder and milk into a bowl and mix with an electric mixer for 2 minutes.

2 Melt the butter and pour into the oven dish. Pour in the batter and then place the plums around the dish, cut side down, on top of the batter.

3 Bake for an hour until golden brown on top.

OPTIONS

Serve with fresh cream, ice-cream or custard.

L: Serve with custard made with low-fat milk.

G-F: see following recipe.

GLUTEN-FREE PLUM COBBLER

Oven 200°C/400°F/gas mark 6

Oven dish 28cm x 20cm x 5cm deep, approx.

INGREDIENTS

6 plums, halved and stoned

25g sugar for the plums

a knob of butter to grease the tin

120g gluten-free Tritamyl flour

120ml sweet, clear, carbonated drink e.g. 7Up

30g caster sugar

40g butter

2 medium eggs, at room temperature and separated

SHOPPING LIST

fresh plums

gluten-free Tritamyl flour

carbonated drink

METHOD

1 Generously grease the oven dish with butter, leaving any extra in the dish. Sprinkle half the sugar onto the dish. Arrange the plums, cut side down on the sugar and sprinkle the rest of the sugar over them.

2 Put the egg whites into a bowl with a pinch of salt and whisk until stiff but glossy.

3 Mix the flour and caster sugar in a bowl and rub the butter in well. Add the egg yolks to the carbonated drink and whisk a little – it's important not to over-whisk. Stir gently into the flour mixture – ignore tiny lumps and don't over-mix.

4 Fold the stiff egg whites carefully into the flour mixture and mix carefully. Again this should be fast and don't worry about small pieces of egg white not being mixed in.

5 Pour over the plums in the dish and bake in the preheated oven for 20-25 minutes, until the batter springs back to the touch. Serve hot or cold as above.

OLD-FASHIONED IRISH APPLE TART

As a child we had a large orchard and, in autumn and early winter, there was always an abundance of fat, green Bramley apples. Mother regularly made apple tarts and had very high standards: she wasn't happy if a little of the apple filling happened to ooze out of the holes in the top and sides of the pastry. These rejects, however, were my favourite tarts, which is probably why I love the French Tarte Tatin with its abundance of delightful caramelised apples. Since I couldn't decide between tarts, I'm including both recipes.

Oven 210°C/410°F/gas mark 6½

INGREDIENTS

For the pastry

170g (1½ cup) flour

85g butter, cold from the fridge – increase to 115g if you like shorter pastry

a little extra butter for greasing the apple dish

¼ tsp salt

cold water

For the filling

2-3 Bramley or other green cooking apples

2-3 tbsp sugar or to taste

2-3 whole cloves (optional)

METHOD

1 Grease an enamel plate, 22-25cm in diameter.

2 Mix the flour and salt together in a bowl and, with a cold knife, cut the butter into the flour in small pieces. Rub the butter into the flour and mix in enough cold water to make a stiff pastry dough. Put into a plastic container or bag and refrigerate for at least 20 minutes before rolling out. (Pastry will keep in the fridge in this way for a few days or can be frozen for up to 6 months.)

3 Peel the apples and cut into quarters. Remove the cores and pips and slice the quarters.

4 Lightly flour a clean worktop or board. Remove the pastry from the fridge and cut in two. Shape one of the pieces into a round ball (keep handling to a minimum) and roll out on the floured board to a circle slightly wider than the tart dish. Roll

the pastry over the rolling pin and carefully place it on the buttered dish

5 Place the sliced apples on top of the pastry and sprinkle the sugar over the top.

6 Wet the edges of the pastry with a pastry brush or your finger.

7 Roll out the second half of the pastry in the same way and cover the apples with it.

8 Press down on the sides which are wet to seal the top and bottom of the tart together. Trim the edges with a knife and then make a design on the edge, by pressing your thumb and a fork alternately into the edges of the pastry. Prick the top of the tart five or six times with a fork.

9 Purists would say that the top of the tart should be as close to white as possible. However, if you like your tart to turn golden, brush it with a little milk or beaten egg.

10 Place the tart in the preheated oven and bake for 10 minutes. Reduce the heat to 170°C/340°F/gas mark 3½ and cook

for about another 30-40 minutes until golden brown on top. The tart can be served either hot or cold.

SHOPPING LIST
2-3 cooking apples, preferably Bramleys
cloves, if using

OPTIONS

Serve hot with cream or ice cream or as an accompaniment to tea or coffee when cold. It can also be served with either hot or cold custard.

L: Serve with low-fat crème fraiche or low-fat ice-cream.

Note: *If you're short of time, this shortcrust pastry can be bought, readymade, in the frozen section of the supermarket. Also, these apple tarts freeze extremely well and, once defrosted, and reheated in the oven, they taste just as good as fresh tarts. See page 230 for pastry-making tips.*

TARTE TATIN AUX POMMES

Oven 190°C/375°F/gas mark 5

Deep sandwich tin, 20cm in diameter, approx.

INGREDIENTS

For the pastry

250g flour

125g butter, cold from the fridge

60g caster sugar

2 egg yolks

a pinch of salt

For the filling

3-4 Bramley or other green cooking apples

60g butter, cold from the fridge

60g brown sugar

SHOPPING LIST

cooking apples, preferably Bramleys

METHOD

Put the flour, sugar and salt into a bowl and, with a cold knife, cut the butter into it in small pieces. Rub the butter into the flour. Make a well in the centre of the flour and mix in the egg yolks to form a fairly stiff dough. The dough should be wet enough to form a ball but dry enough so as not to stick to the sides of the bowl. If it's too crumbly, add a tiny bit of very cold water. Try to handle the pastry as little as possible as excessive handling makes it tough. Put it into a plastic bag or container and refrigerate for at least 20 minutes before rolling out. (The pastry can be stored in the fridge for a few days or can be frozen for up to 6 months.)

2 Put half the sugar for the filling in the sandwich tin and place on the hob over a low heat until the sugar caramelises a little.

3 Peel and quarter the apples and remove the cores and pips. Slice thinly and arrange in circles in the tin. Sprinkle the rest of the sugar over the apples and dot with the butter.

4 On a lightly floured board, roll out the pastry, a little bigger than the size of the tin and place over the apples, tucking the extra down the insides of the tin.

5 Bake for about 45 minutes or until golden brown on top.

6 Remove from the oven, place a plate over the tin and turn upside down on to the plate. Can be served hot or cold.

OPTIONS

Serve hot with cream or ice-cream or as an accompaniment to tea or coffee when cold. It can also be served with either hot or cold custard.

L: Serve with low-fat crème fraiche or low-fat ice cream.

G-F: Replace the flour in the above recipe with the same quantity of gluten-free flour, add 1 tsp Xanthan gum and proceed as above.

CRANBERRY PINEAPPLE

This is a great recipe for around Christmas time when you feel you've eaten too much and you want something a little lighter but with a bit of sting. It's also a great way to use up the fresh cranberries with which you had planned to make cranberry sauce and didn't. It can be changed into a summer or an autumn dessert too, by replacing the cranberries with whatever is in season: blackberries, strawberries, raspberries, blueberries. It can be served hot or cold.

Oven 180°C/350°F/gas mark 4

INGREDIENTS

8 pineapple rings in syrup, approx. 280g drained weight (reserve the juice from the tin)

60g sugar

60ml water

a squeeze of lemon juice

2 tsp icing sugar

½ cup of fresh cranberries

60ml white rum, or about half a wine glass

SHOPPING LIST

tinned pineapple
fresh cranberries
white rum

METHOD

Drain the pineapples and put the liquid into a saucepan. Add the sugar, water and lemon juice and place over a medium heat, stirring until the sugar dissolves. Increase the heat and bring to the boil. Boil rapidly for about 5 minutes until a little thicker and more syrupy. Cool a little and add the rum.

2 Put the pineapple rings in a ceramic oven dish and pour the syrup over them. Sprinkle the cranberries over the pineapples and place in the preheated oven. Bake for 40 minutes.

3 Heat the grill to maximum.

4 Sprinkle the icing sugar over the pineapples and place under the hot grill. Grill until the sugar caramelises to a golden brown colour.

OPTIONS

They can be served on their own, or with fresh cream, custard, ice-cream or all of the above.

L: Reduce the syrup by half and serve the slices on their own, without cream or custard.

C-F: Chop up the pineapples into small pieces and mix with custard or ice-cream.

G-F: Ensure that the icing sugar is gluten-free.

MERINGUE-TOPPED TAPIOCA PUDDING

This is distinctly different from plain old boiled tapioca. It's a deliciously light pudding, topped with fluffy meringue, which suits any dinner table from everyday to the most formal – and it's a very low-cost dessert! The pudding can also be made without the meringue topping.

Oven 170°C/340°F/gas mark 3½

Pie dish approx. 24cm x 26cm x 5cm

INGREDIENTS

80g tapioca, washed

1 litre milk

15g butter plus extra to generously grease the pie dish

45g sugar, for the tapioca (this will make the tapioca quite sweet and can be reduced or increased to taste)

30g caster sugar, for the meringue

3 large eggs, separated

1 tsp vanilla essence

grated rind of 1 lemon

SHOPPING LIST

tapioca

METHOD

1 Drain the rinsed tapioca. Place it in a stainless steel saucepan with the milk and leave to soak for 2 hours. Then add half the butter and bring to the boil, stirring frequently. Reduce the heat to a very low simmer and cook until the grains are soft, stirring frequently. This can take up to an hour. If you have a ceramic hob you can turn off the heat altogether, at this point and leave it to finish cooking on the warm hob.

2 Whisk in the sugar, egg yolks, lemon rind, vanilla essence and the rest of the butter until just mixed, and pour into the buttered pie dish. Place the pie dish in a deep oven dish that's at least 3cm wider all around. Add boiling water to the larger dish and bake the pudding in the preheated oven until set – about an hour.

3 Meanwhile whisk the egg whites until stiff and fold into the caster sugar. (When folding anything into whipped egg whites, it's best to add the whites to the sugar – i.e. always have the heaviest item on the bottom to minimise air loss.) Pour the meringue mixture over the tapioca, and spread evenly and quickly, using light movements to avoid air loss.

4 Reduce the oven temperature to 150°C/300°F/gas mark 2. Return the pudding, without the outer dish, to the oven and bake until the meringue is golden brown – about 30 minutes. The pudding can be served hot or cold.

OPTIONS

Serve on its own or with fresh, whipped cream.

L: Use low-fat milk, leave out the butter in the tapioca and serve without cream.

> **Note:** *The tapioca grains are small so use a very fine sieve to drain the tapioca or it will all go down the plughole.*
> *For best results, eggs should be at room temperature.*

FRESH FRUIT SALAD

Fresh fruit salad is the perfect 'one size fits all' dessert. It can follow most main courses with aplomb and contains enough healthy fresh fruit to salve the conscience pangs of having a dessert. The salad can be varied with the seasons and what is on offer. I usually make a simple sugar syrup as a base and add different flavourings according to the fruit available and my mood.

INGREDIENTS

Basic sugar syrup

500ml water

75g sugar

juice of 1 lemon (I usually put in the grated rind too)

2 tbsp sherry (optional)

Suggested fruit combinations

Old-fashioned: apples, oranges, pears, grapes, bananas

Green: apples, grapes, kiwis, lime

Minted melon: watermelon, cantaloupe melon, honeydew melon, lime, kirsch (optional)

SHOPPING LIST

sherry, optional
fruit of choice
kirsch (optional)
fresh mint, if using

METHOD

1 Wash and chop the fruit into a bowl – see below for fruit combinations. The fruit can be peeled but I like to leave the skin on, for taste, colour and crunch.

2 Put the water, sugar and lemon rind, if using, into a saucepan and stir over a medium heat until the sugar dissolves. Bring to the boil and boil until the syrup reduces by half. Remove from the heat and add the lemon juice. Traditionally the hot syrup was poured over the prepared fruit with enough syrup to cover the fruit. I use just enough syrup to cover a third to half of the fruit. I also like my fruit salad to retain its crunch so I let the syrup cool before pouring it over the fruit.

3 Allow to cool and then refrigerate for 2 hours before serving.

Note on suggested fruit combinations:

Old-fashioned: *Remove all pith from the oranges as it makes the salad bitter. Add the bananas just before serving.*

Green: *Replace the lemon in the syrup with lime.*

Minted melon: *Replace the lemon in the syrup with lime. This can be served in the skins of the honeydew and cantaloupe melons – choose melons of roughly the same size. A little kirsch is good in this one.*

OPTIONS

Undo all the good work of choosing a relatively healthy dessert and serve with fresh cream and/or ice-cream.

L: Reduce the sugar to 40g and omit the cream. Serve low-fat ice cream.

C-F: Peel the fruit and cut it into small pieces, about 1cm square. Omit the alcohol and mint and serve with ice-cream.

POIRES BELLE HÉLÈNE

This was once a very popular dessert but fashions in food, like clothes and furniture, change. It is very easy to make, economical and combines three of my favourite things: fruit, chocolate and ice-cream. If in haste, use tinned pears.

INGREDIENTS

4 pears, peeled, cored and halved

250g sugar

500ml water

juice of half a lemon

250ml cream

300g plain chocolate

vanilla ice cream to serve

SHOPPING LIST

pears
cream
plain chocolate ice-cream

METHOD

1 Put the sugar and water into a saucepan and heat, stirring until the sugar dissolves. Add the lemon juice and the pear halves (assuming you are using fresh pears) and simmer for 10-15 minutes, turning halfway through, until the pears are tender. Remove the pears from the syrup and set aside, with the syrup, to cool.

2 Put the cream into a saucepan and heat slowly, being careful not to let it boil or simmer. Break the chocolate into it, in pieces, and stir until it dissolves. Finally add 25ml of the syrup used to cook the pears and stir well.

3 Put a large scoop of ice cream into each dessert dish, cover on each side with a pear half, and pour chocolate sauce over one of the pear halves. Serve immediately.

OPTIONS

Serve as is or with whipped cream and a sweet biscuit such as a nougatine. A sprinkling of toasted slivered almonds is also good.

L: Reduce the sugar content of the poaching syrup to 175g. Instead of all cream, use 125ml low-fat milk and 125ml of cream for the sauce.

C-F: When serving, chop the pear halves and serve with half the amount of chocolate sauce.

G-F: Ensure the chocolate and ice-cream are gluten-free.

CARAMELISED FRESH FRUIT WITH CRÈME FRAICHE

Grilled fruit has to be one of the most simple yet scrumptious of desserts. Plums, peaches, nectarines and pears are my favourites. Prepare the fruit earlier and leave in the fridge. After your main course, just pop them under the grill for 3 or 4 minutes and they're ready.

INGREDIENTS

2 peaches

2 nectarines

2 plums

2 small pears

2 tbsp icing sugar and about ½ tbsp more to serve

300ml crème fraiche, to serve

SHOPPING LIST

peaches

nectarines

plums

pears

crème fraiche, to serve

METHOD

1 Quarter the pears and remove the core and pips. Halve the rest of the fruit and remove the pips. Place the fruit on an ovenproof, earthenware plate or shallow dish, skin side down, and sprinkle 1 tbsp sugar over them. Put them into the fridge for about 15 minutes, by which time the sugar will have melted into the fruit.

2 Heat the grill to maximum.

3 Sprinkle another tbsp of icing sugar over the fruit and place under the grill. Cook for 3-4 minutes until brown and caramelised on top.

4 Divide the fruit between four dessert dishes, sprinkle with the remaining icing sugar and serve with the crème fraiche.

OPTIONS

Cream or vanilla ice cream can be substituted for the crème fraiche.

L: Use low-fat crème fraiche.

C-F: Chop the grilled fruit into small pieces and serve with vanilla ice cream.

G-F: Make sure the icing sugar used is gluten-free.

SHREWD
KITCHEN AND
COOKING TIPS

Following are some tips that I've gathered over the years. They can help you to avoid pitfalls, be economical and save time in the kitchen.

PERFECT HARD-BOILED EGGS

Do the 'witch' test to tell if an egg is fresh or not. Put it into a bowl of cold, salted water. If it sinks, it's fresh.

1 Place eggs in a single layer in a saucepan, Cover with water plus about 2cm extra. Bring to the boil, uncovered, and boil for one minute.

2 Remove from heat, cover and leave for 10 minutes.

3 Drain and put into a bowl of very cold water and leave for 5 minutes. Peel and use as desired. If you do not want to use them immediately, leave unpeeled and refrigerate. They will keep for up to a week in the fridge.

STIR-FRYING

Make sure the oil is hot enough – heat until it starts to smoke and then wait another 20-30 seconds. When stir-frying vegetables, start stirring immediately; when stir-frying meat, wait for about a minute before you stir.

When stir-frying a meat and vegetable dish, start with the vegetables that take the longest to cook, followed by the other vegetables. Remove the vegetables and set aside. The meat should be cooked last.

Avoid over-cooking vegetables. They need to retain their colour and some crunch. The last thing you want is a lot of limp vegetables on a plate.

HOMEMADE STOCK

Making your own stock is not the chore it might seem: it's mostly a matter of throwing the ingredients in a pot or casserole and cooking them for a few hours. But the effort pays big dividends in terms of taste. I prefer to make mine in the oven as this controls the temperature and I can forget about it for a few hours. It's a good idea to make a double batch and freeze it for later use. If freezer space is an issue, you can boil the finished stock in an uncovered saucepan until it's reduced by half and freeze it in smaller cartons or even in ice cube trays. To make maximum use of oven heat, please see the list at the end of the chicken stock recipes for other recipes that can be cooked at the same time.

CHICKEN STOCK

INGREDIENTS

1kg raw or cooked chicken bones (when roasting chicken it's a good idea to freeze the carcass until you have a few and then use them for stock)

1 onion, peeled and sliced

2 sticks of celery, chopped

1 large carrot, chopped

1 bay leaf

a sprig of fresh thyme

salt and black pepper

METHOD

1 If using the oven method, preheat the oven to 180°C/350°F/gas mark 4.

2 Put all the ingredients into an ovenproof pot or flameproof casserole. Cover with cold water and bring just to the boil. Skim the top and bring to a simmer. Cover and place in the preheated oven, or simmer on the hob, for about 4 hours.

3 At the end of the cooking time, skim any fat and scum from the top and strain the stock.

4 This will yield about 500ml of stock and can be kept in the fridge for 3-5 days or frozen for up to 3 months.

VEGETABLE STOCK

This is a basic vegetable stock recipe that can be used as a base for many recipes, such as soups and sauces.

INGREDIENTS

2 medium onions, chopped

4 carrots, chopped

3 celery sticks, chopped

1oz butter or 2 tbsp sunflower or corn oil

1 tsp dried mixed herbs

2 litres cold water

salt and white pepper to season

METHOD

1 Heat the butter or oil in a pan. Add the chopped onion and cook gently until the onions are transparent. Add the other vegetables and stir.

2 Cook gently for about 15 minutes, being careful that the vegetables do not brown. Add the herbs, water and seasoning and bring to a gentle simmer. Simmer for about 45 minutes and strain.

OTHER RECIPES THAT CAN BE COOKED AT THE SAME TIME AS THE STOCK:

Yoghurt Chicken (page 52)
Red Pepper Chicken Baskets (page 30)
Trout en Papillote (page 186)
Clementine Clafoutis (page 202)
Irish Whiskey Baked Apples (page 208)
Old-Fashioned Irish Apple Tart (page 212)
Meringue-Topped Tapioca Pudding (page 218)

BOILED RICE

There are many different types of rice and many different ways to cook them. To simplify things here, we are going to cook only two types – basmati (good with curries of all kinds) and long grain rice.

Long Grain Rice

1 For 4 people, rinse two cups of rice in a strainer and soak in cold water for 30 minutes. Drain thoroughly. Heat ½ to 1 tbsp sunflower or corn oil in a saucepan and add the rice. Stir and add two cups of cold water and ½ tsp salt.

2 Cover with a lid and bring to a vigorous boil. Stir well, making sure none of the rice is sticking to the bottom of the pot. Turn off the heat if using an electric cooker. For gas cookers, stir and keep on the lowest heat possible for about 5 minutes and then turn off the heat.

3 Leave for another 10 minutes and then stir gently to separate the grains. Leave for another 10 minutes and stir gently again. The rice is now ready to serve.

Basmati Rice

A good quality basmati rice will not need soaking and can be cooked as above leaving out the soaking process.

PASTRY-MAKING TIPS

Good pastry needs cold hands so run your hands under cold water before you begin. An alternative to this is to freeze the butter a few hours before you start and grate the frozen butter. Then rub this into the flour thoroughly but quickly, so as not to give the butter time to start to melt. Then finish off your pastry in the normal way.

Handle the pastry as little as possible. After mixing the pastry, refrigerate for at least 20 minutes, to allow the pastry to rest before using. This stops it from springing back when you start to roll it.

CHOPPING CHILLIES

Chopping hot chillies can leave a residue on your fingers, which may cause the skin to burn and can be very unpleasant and even painful if you happen to rub your eyes. To avoid this, rub your fingers with a little oil before you chop chillies and wash hands thoroughly afterwards.

HOW TO MAKE BREADCRUMBS

Fresh bread, which has been dried, makes the best crumbs. For all-purpose breadcrumbs, I find batch loaf is tastiest. Preheat the oven to 140°C/275°F/gas mark 1. Slice the bread thinly and place on an oven tray. Bake until dry – about 20 minutes – turning after 10 minutes so that the slices dry evenly. Then crumb by hand or in a food processor. An alternative to this is to crush them with a rolling pin, and a neat way to save mess when doing this, is to pop the dried bread into a strong paper or plastic bag and crush them in the bag.

To make toasted breadcrumbs, simply toast the bread on a low setting until dry and golden. If your toaster does not have a low enough setting for this, you may have to toast the bread, allow it to cool and repeat the process so that the bread becomes dry without burning. Toasted breadcrumbs can be too hard to crumb by hand, so you may need to use either a rolling pin or a food processor.

Different types of bread can be used for breadcrumbs, and can even be mixed together for a variety of different tastes. One of my favourites, especially for fish dishes, is toasted pitta bread crumbs.

It is not economical to make a small quantity of breadcrumbs at a time, so it's a good idea to make a lot and freeze them in small bags. They last about six months in the freezer.

COOKING VEGETABLES

If your vegetables are cooking too fast and are going to be ready before the rest of the meal, plunge them into cold water. Five minutes before serving, add boiling water and simmer for a couple of minutes to heat through.

GREASY GRAVY

If your gravy is greasy, add a little lemon juice. This will give it flavour and reduce the greasy taste. Or throw in some ice cubes – the fat will stick to the cubes and can then be removed.

JUICY LEMONS

To get more juice from lemons, bring them to room temperature and roll them on a board or the kitchen counter with your palm before cutting.

KEEPING SALT DRY

Add a few grains of dessert rice to the salt cellar to prevent the salt from getting damp.

HOW TO SKIN A FISH

Place the fish skin side down on the chopping board. Starting at the tail, cut through the flesh as far as, but not through, the skin. Turn the knife at an angle pointing between the skin and the flesh, and away from your other hand. With a back and forth movement, pushing against the skin a little, cut the flesh away from the skin.

HOW TO SHELL A LOBSTER

First twist the claws to break them off. Cover the claws with a clean tea towel and crush with a mallet or a lobster cracker. Remove the pieces of shell and scoop the meat out. Turn the underside of the lobster uppermost and, with a sharp knife, cut it in half from head to tail. Pull the shell apart and remove the meat. If there is a black vein along the centre of the tail, remove this and discard. Remove the head and stomach and other soft parts, and discard.

KEEPING COFFEE FRESH

Keep freshly ground coffee in the freezer to preserve its taste.

SHREWD
FREEZING

I cannot stress enough the advantages of a freezer when applying the shrewd method. I regularly take advantage of special offers on meat and fish and store them in the freezer, and I also batch cook dishes: some for now, some for later. Not only does this save money, but on busy days it's great to have a cooked meal already prepared that can be defrosted and reheated with minimum time and effort.

In this chapter you will find some tips to help you make the right choice of freezer for your needs, and some guidelines on how to use it for maximum benefit.

BUYING A FREEZER

There are many advantages to freezing food. Top of my list are the saving of time and money. I find a big freezer invaluable and, if you have the space, it's a shrewd investment that won't take long to pay dividends. There are currently two types of freezer on the market, upright and chest, and listed below are some of the advantages and disadvantages of each.

Chest Freezer

ADVANTAGES

*   They are often more energy efficient, and this is becoming increasingly important in the light of global warming and carbon taxes.

*   They stay cold longer if there's a power cut.

*   They are often less expensive than upright models.

DISADVANTAGES

*   Access to items at the bottom of the chest can be difficult and involves taking out items on top. This is time-consuming, and can be difficult or even impossible for the elderly or those with physical disabilities.

*   Many chest freezers are not lit inside so it can be hard to see the contents.

Upright Freezer

ADVANTAGES

*   It's easy to see the contents and access the different sections.

*   The shelving system makes it easy to organise the contents.

DISADVANTAGES

*   They are usually more expensive to buy than chest freezers

*   They are less energy efficient as more cold air escapes when the door is opened.

The size of the freezer is the next thing to decide. Things to take into consideration here are the number of people it will be servicing, what you will use it for - for example will you just store food until the next shop, or will it be used for storing bulk buys and batches of cooked food? Or perhaps you will need to store items that you cannot source locally, or make a trip to your favourite organic butcher and buy a side of beef. The space available for your freezer in your kitchen or utility room (or even your garage) also needs to be taken into account.

The other big consideration before you make your purchase is whether to buy a frost-free or manual defrost model. The former is usually more noisy but you never have to defrost it so it saves time and hassle. Frost-free freezers are, however, usually more expensive to buy, but it is very convenient not to have to empty out and defrost the freezer.

If you are buying a fridge-freezer, it is more convenient to have the freezer on the bottom, so that you are not constantly bending down to get things from the fridge.

And finally, look at the energy rating – an A-rated appliance can use up to 50 per cent less energy than a G-rated appliance. It is interesting to note that American-style fridge-freezers can be a lot more energy hungry than a regular fridge-freezer. (Source: Sustainable Energy Ireland, www.sei.ie.)

FREEZING GUIDELINES & TIPS

Most freezers come with a booklet containing guidelines for safety and storage times for various foods, and it is essential to follow the manufacturer's guidelines, not only from a health perspective but also to ensure that the quality of the food is retained.

Here are some general tips to enable you to get the most from your freezer:

1 Store everything in airtight containers to protect the food and avoid moisture loss.

2 Supermarket wrapping is fine for short-term freezing of up to a couple of months, but food that is to be stored for longer should be placed in freezer bags or containers.

3 Label all foods showing contents and date frozen.

4 Liquids expand when frozen, so leave a little extra space for this in the freezer container.

5 Do not leave empty spaces in your freezer. Fill plastic containers with water and put them in the empty spaces – this will help keep your freezer cold and save on electricity.

6 Buy several items of a special offer and freeze them for later use, either cooked or uncooked.

7 Don't throw leftovers away – freeze them for use at a later stage.

8 For best results, thaw food in the fridge.

9 Foods which don't freeze well include eggs, lettuce, radishes, uncooked potatoes, aubergines, spring onions, courgettes, cabbage and uncooked fruit such as apples, apricots, peaches, plums and rhubarb.

RECOMMENDED FOOD FREEZING TIMES

Once frozen and maintained in its frozen state, frozen food will always be safe. However, the quality of frozen food deteriorates over time. The better the quality and freshness of the food at the time of freezing, the better it will taste when defrosted.

Many food labels contain guidelines for freezing. The table opposite lists recommended times for freezing selected food items. These are general guidelines only, consult your own freezer handbook for further information.

ITEM	DURATION	ITEM	DURATION
Meat and Poultry			
Bacon	1 to 2 months	Plaice	10 months
Beef minced	3 to 4 months	Prawns	6 months
Beef roasts	6 to 12 months	Salmon	4 months
Beef steaks	6 to 12 months	**Dairy Products**	
Chicken	9 months		
Lamb chops	6 to 9 months	Butter and margarine	6 to 9 months
Lamb minced	3 to 4 months	Cheese – hard	6 months
Lamb roasts	6 to 9 months	Cheese – soft	1 months
Pork chops	4 to 6 months	Cream	Up to 1 month
Pork minced	3 to 4 months	Egg wihtes	12 months
Pork roasts	4 to 6 months	Milk	Up to 1 month
Sausages	1 to 2 months	**Cooked Food**	
Stewing meats	3 to 4 months		
Turkey	9 months	Casseroles	2 to 3 months
Veal roasts	4 to 6 months	Fish	2 to 3 months
Fish		Frozen dinners	3 to 4 months
Cod	8 months	Gravy	2 to 3 months
Haddock	8 months	Ham	1 to 3 months
Herring	4 months	Meat	2 to 3 months
Mackerel	4 months	Soups	2 to 3 months
		Stews	2 to 3 months

SHREWD
ENERGY

Energy is very newsworthy at the moment, but whatever the source, be it electricity, gas, wind, sun, oil or solid fuel, it all costs. Whilst for most people, the energy saved on cooking will not be great compared with the the energy that can be saved on heating and light, it is still worth considering in terms of long-term cost savings and carbon emissions.

If you are refitting your kitchen it's important to choose appliances that are energy-efficient. And it's interesting to note that vegetables generally cook a lot faster than meat, so by reducing your meat and increasing your vegetable intake, you will not only be healthier but will also save money in the cooking process.

EASY WAYS OF SAVING ENERGY IN COOKING

* **PUT A LID ON IT**

Putting a lid on a saucepan traps the heat and the contents cook faster, using less energy.

* **USE LESS WATER**

When boiling vegetables use a minimal amount of water, but do keep an eye on them as the water can easily boil away and the vegetables will burn. When boiling the kettle for tea or coffee, only boil the amount of water needed – most modern electric kettles have the heating element at the bottom so that a small amount of water can be boiled.

* **POT SIZE = HEAT SOURCE**

The pot should not be smaller than the cooker ring as the extra heat is wasted. If using gas, the flame should not come up the sides of the pot.

* **ALL IN ONE**

Cooking everything in one pot saves energy and is ideal for stews, casseroles and biryanis. There are dividers available for pots so that different things can be cooked in the same pot. Layered steamers also work well, especially for vegetables. And the all-in-one approach is great, too, when it comes to washing up!

* **NO PEEPING!**

Avoid opening the oven door unnecessarily to look at how the food is progressing. This can be lethal for cakes and sponges, as sudden cold air early on in the cooking process can cause them to flop. It also results in rapid loss of heat, which is expensive and will slow up the cooking process. If you have a see-through door on the oven, use that instead. If you need to work on the food that's cooking in the oven, e.g. basting, remove the food and work on it outside the oven, keeping the oven door closed in the meantime to conserve heat.

* **KEEP PREHEATING TIME TO A MINIMUM**

Many recipes instruct that the oven be turned on before the start of food preparation. This is often unnecessary as food preparation can take much longer than it takes for the oven to heat up. Time how long it takes to prepare food for the oven, and how long it usually takes for the oven to reach the required temperature, so that you can synchronise the two.

* **SELF-CLEANING OVENS**

The self-cleaning facility in an oven uses a lot of power. Avoid using it a lot and, when you do, use it after you have cooked something to take advantage of the residual heat. Wiping the inside of the oven with a damp cloth while it is still warm (not hot) will keep it clean for longer.

* **HAVE BIG COOK-UPS**

Cooking larger batches of food, whether on the hob or in the oven, saves energy. The extra quantities can be frozen for consumption at a later date. In Egypt, it is common for women to have a big cook-up once a week for the week ahead, and then refrigerate or freeze the extra food. When using the oven, make full use of the heat by cooking a few things together. However, care should be taken here to avoid filling the shelves too much, as this can restrict air flow and cause uneven temperatures. Avoid covering oven trays with tinfoil for the same reason.

* **MICROWAVE**

Use the microwave to cook and reheat food. While they use considerable amounts of electricity, they more than make up for it in reduced cooking time.

* **USE A PRESSURE COOKER**

They cook food, especially cheaper cuts of meat, significantly faster. I find my pressure cooker great for tougher cuts of meat and I usually cook ham and bacon in it.

* **USE A CROCKPOT**

Crockpots (slow cookers) cook food at very low temperatures for long periods and most are very energy efficient. Like pressure cookers, they can make cheaper, tougher cuts of meat deliciously tender. They are also great for those who are out at work during the day. Turn on in the morning before you go to work, and dinner will be ready when you get back home.

I'm a firm believer in moderation in all things, so I don't think it's a good idea to go overboard on energy-saving while cooking. Cooking should be fun and spontaneous, but it is good to be aware of how we can save energy in the home. After a little initial effort, thought and practice, energy-saving habits becoming second nature.

OVEN TEMPERATURE CHART

Oven temperatures given are for fan-assisted ovens – temperatures for a non-fan-assisted oven will vary according to the type used, but as a rough guide, should be increased by about 10-20 degrees celsius or 20-35 degrees Fahrenheit.

GAS MARK	FAHRENHEIT	CELSIUS	DESCRIPTION
¼	225	110	Very cool/very slow
½	250	125	–
1	275	140	Cool
2	300	150	–
3	325	165	Very moderate
4	350	180	Moderate
5	375	190	–
6	400	200	Moderately hot
7	425	220	Hot
8	450	230	–
9	475	240	Very hot

ACKNOWLEDGEMENTS

A lot of man- and woman-hours went into the writing of this book and it would not have been possible without the help of the following people: My son Omar, who tirelessly researched and built the shrewdfood.ie website and continues to update, revamp and take photographs, and who is always supportive and upbeat.

My partner Tom who has taken photos, tasted, given feedback and supported the project often into the small hours of the morning.

My friends who allowed me to include their recipes for their support.

Breda Purdue of Hachette Books Ireland who gave me the opportunity to write this book and all the Hachette team, especially my editor Ciara Considine whose input has been very helpful.